TOP 50

Bible Stories about Jesus

FOR ELEMENTARY

ROSEKiDZ®

Top 50 Bible Stories about Jesus for Elementary

Published by RoseKidz®
an imprint of Hendrickson Publishing Group
Rose Publishing, LLC
P.O. Box 3473
Peabody, Massachusetts 01961-3473 USA
www.hendricksonpublishinggroup.com

Managing Editor: Karen McGraw
Editorial and Production Associate: Drew McCall
Assistant Editor: Talia Messina

Cover & Interior Design: Drew McCall
New material written by Drew McCall

ISBN: 978-1-62862-974-3
RoseKidz® reorder# 629745
Product Code: R50026
RELIGION/Christian Ministry/Children

Printed in United States of America
Printed November 2020

Table of Contents

Jesus' Birth and Childhood

Jesus' Life & Ministry

Jesus' Last Days, Death, & Resurrection

Section 1

Jesus' Birth & Childhood

A Savior Is Coming

✓

Chapter 1

Memory verse 📖

She will give birth to a son and will call him Immanuel (which means "God is with us"). — *memory verse*
Isaiah 7:14

God Keeps His Promises (based on Isaiah 7:14; Micah 5:2)

Have you ever heard of a prophet? A prophet is someone who speaks for God and gives his message to others. Do you know about any prophets from the Bible? In the Old Testament, God chose people to share his message with those around them.

God spoke directly through the prophets to announce the coming of the Messiah. Isaiah and Micah are two prophets we read about in the Old Testament. God told these men that he was sending a Messiah to be their ruler. Because these were prophecies from God, they were all fulfilled. God always keeps his promises.

Old Testament prophets told about the birth of a Messiah years before it happened. Isaiah prophesied that a child would be born to a virgin. Micah prophesied that the Messiah would be born in Bethlehem.

Isaiah also prophesied what Jesus' name would be. In Matthew 1:23 the prophecy is repeated. The special name they would call Jesus means "God with us." — His Name was Emmanuel

Discussion

questions 💬

1. What did the prophets say Jesus' name would mean? — God with us.
2. How did God keep his promise through the prophets? —

Prophecy and Its Fulfillment Match

X not this

what you need ✏

- Crayons or markers

what you do ✂

Before class, photocopy this page, making one for each child.

what children do ✋

1. Draw a line from the prophecy on the left to its correct fulfillment on the right.

what to say 📢

Every prophecy that was told by the prophets came true. Read the statements and Scriptures on the right and draw a line to the prophecy that was fulfilled.

1. The Messiah would be born to a virgin. (Isaiah 7:14)	Luke 2:4
2. The Messiah would be born in Bethlehem. (Micah 5:2)	Luke 22:47-48
3. The Messiah would suffer rejection by his own people. (Psalm 69:8)	John 1:11
4. The Messiah would perform many miracles. (Isaiah 35:5, 6)	Mark 15:27
5. The Messiah would be betrayed by a friend. (Psalm 41:9)	Matthew 28:6
6. The Messiah would be crucified between two thieves. (Isaiah 53:12)	Luke 1:27
7. The Messiah would be raised from the dead. (Psalm 16:10)	Matthew 11:5

Name Scramble

older kids

what you need ✏️

- Crayons or markers

what you do ✂️

Before class, photocopy this page, making one for each child.

what children do ✋

1. Unscramble the words below to see the different names for Jesus. Look up each Scripture reference for a hint.

what to say 📢

Messiah means anointed one, or someone set apart for a particular service. Can you unscramble the letters below to find out some of the other names the Messiah was called? The Scripture references are included in case you need a hint.

1. SEUJS (Matthew 1:25) _____

2. RBDAE FO FEIL (John 6:35) _____

3. HET OGDO PSEHDHER (John 10:11) _____

4. EATG (John 10:9) _____

5. WDOR (John 1:1) _____

6. HET IGLTH FO HET DLWRO (John 8:12) _____

7. VRSAIO (John 4:42) _____

8. HET RUET RGNEPVEAI (John 15:1) _____

The Prophet's Path

what you need 🖌

- Crayons or markers

what you do ✂

Before class, photocopy this page, making one for each child.

what children do ✋

1. Use crayons or markers to follow the path to Bethlehem.

what to say 📢

Follow the prophet to see if Micah's prophecy was fulfilled.

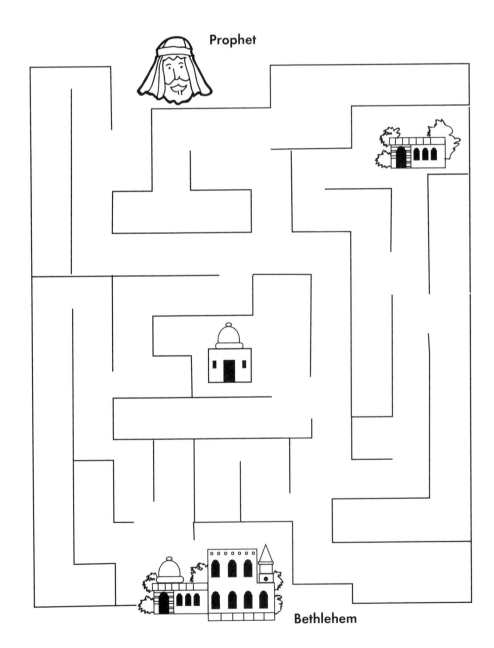

Prophet

Bethlehem

A Savior Is Coming *not this*

God Keeps His Promises (based on Isaiah 7:14; Micah 5:2)

memory verse 📖

She will give birth to a son and will call him Immanuel (which means "God is with us").
Isaiah 7:14

discussion questions 💬

1. What did the prophets say Jesus' name would mean?
2. How did God keep his promise through the prophets?

Find that Name

Use the letter dial to find the name Isaiah said would be one of Jesus' names. The letters under the blanks refer to the letters in the outside circle. On the blank, write the letter on the inside circle that is directly under the outside letter. Then color the picture of baby Jesus.

Start

___ ___ ___ ___ ___ ___ ___ ___
 T   X   X   L   Y   F   P   W

The Angels' Good News

memory verse

The Lord is with you!
Luke 1:28

Angels Sing of Jesus' Birth (based on Luke 1:26–28)

One day God asked his special messenger angel to tell people that his Son, Jesus, was coming to Earth to be the Savior of the world! Imagine how happy the angel was to announce that wonderful news. Imagine how surprised Mary and Joseph were to see the angel.

The angel carried some important news to the town of Nazareth. The angel told Mary that God wanted her to be the mother of his Son. At first, Mary was afraid. Then what happened?

The angel told Joseph that God wanted him to take care of Mary and her baby boy, Jesus. Did Joseph obey God? Yes.

God still speaks to us today, asking us to hear and obey him. He asks us to tell others the Good News, too.

discussion questions

1. Why did an angel visit Mary and Joseph?
2. How would you feel if you were Mary or Joseph? How would you have responded?

Angel Mosaic

what you need ✒

- Crayons or markers
- Scissors
- Glue
- Construction paper
- Hole punch
- Yarn

what you do ✂

Before class, photocopy this page, making one for each child.

what children do 🖐

1. Use the color code to color the picture.
2. Cut out the angel mosaic.
3. Glue the mosaic onto construction paper, leaving space at the top for a hole.
4. Punch a hole at the top center of the construction paper.
5. Tie yarn through the hole. Hang the mosaic somewhere public to remind you of Jesus' good news.

what to say 📢

The angels must have been so excited to share the news of Jesus' birth. Color this picture to remember that you can share the news of Jesus, too.

1= pink   2=white   3=yellow   4=blue

Good News Crossword

what you need
- Bibles
- Pencils

older kids don't do

what you do
Before class, photocopy this page, making one for each child.

what children do

1. Read each crossword clue. Then, look up and read the verse in parentheses beside it to find the answers.
2. Fill in the correct answers to the crossword.

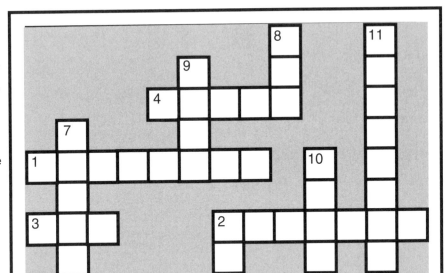

Across
1. God sent an angel to the city of _____ (Luke 1:26).
2. The angel's name was _____ (Luke 1:26).
3. The angel said that Mary would have a _____ (Luke 1:31).
4. Mary's child would rule over the throne of _____ (Luke 1:32).
5. The angel said, "with God _____ shall be impossible" (Luke 1:37).
6. The angel also went to visit _____ (Matthew 1:24).

Down
2. Nazareth was located in _____ (Luke 1:26).
7. The angel told Mary that she had found _____ with God. (Luke 1:30).
8. Mary's baby would be the Son of _____ (Luke 1:35).
9. The angel told Joseph that Jesus "shall _____ His people from their sins" (Matthew 1:21).
10. The prophets had received this message from the _____ (Matthew 1:22).
11. Mary and Joseph both "_____ in God" (Luke 1:47).

What Did the Angel Say?

what you need ✎
- Pencils

— Read to Kids   Play True or False

what you do ✂
Before class, photocopy this page, making one for each child.

what children do ✋
1. Read the following sentences.
2. If the statement is true, write *T* for *true* in the angel. If the statement is false, write *F* for *false* in the angel.

 1. God sent an angel named Michael to visit Mary.

 2. The angel told Mary that God had chosen her to sew a flag for the town of Nazareth.

 3. Mary was afraid when she first heard the angel's news.

 4. The angel told Mary her son would be called the Son of God.

 5. God can do some amazing things, but other things are impossible for God to do.

 6. Mary asked for some time to decide if she would obey God.

 7. The angel appeared to Joseph in his carpenter shop.

 8. The angel told Joseph to let the priests choose a name for Mary's baby.

 9. Joseph saw the angel in a cloud.

 **10.** God told the prophets long ago about this special child's birth.

 11. The special child would save God's people from a big landslide.

 12. The child's name would mean "God with us."

The Angels' Good News

Angels Sing of Jesus' Birth (Luke 1:26–28)

memory verse 📖

The Lord is with you!
Luke 1:28

let kids fill in the pictures (while you read the) words

discussion questions 💬

1. What did the angel tell Mary?
2. How would you feel if you were Mary or Joseph? How would you have responded?

Angel Picture Story

The angel told Joseph that God wanted him to take care of Mary and her baby boy, Jesus. Did Joseph obey God? Read the story and find out! Use the picture. Then tell the story to a friend.

The 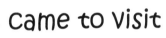 came to visit 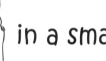 in a small  called

Nazareth. The told  ,"U will have a boy.

U will call him 'Jesus!'" At first was afraid.

Then said, "I will obey God." The also spoke

to . " will have a  boy. Take good care of

and her boy." said, "I will obey God."

Mary Visits Elizabeth

memory verse 📖

Oh, how my soul praises the Lord. How my spirit rejoices in God my Savior!
Luke 1:46–47

A Song of Praise (Based on Luke 1:39–56)

One night an angel visited a woman named Mary and told her she would have a baby. Not only that, the angel told Mary that her baby would be Jesus, the Savior the world had been waiting for.

Mary was so excited. She hurried to Judea to visit Elizabeth, her relative. When Mary greeted Elizabeth, who was also pregnant, the Bible says "Elizabeth's child leaped within her, and Elizabeth was filled with the Holy Spirit." The news of Jesus' arrival was so powerful, even before he was born!

Elizabeth was also carrying a special baby. Her son would be John the Baptist, who preached the good news of Jesus and baptized people in his name. Elizabeth told Mary that she was blessed because she listened to God and believed. Mary responded by praising God for what he had done. She sang a song of praise because God keeps his promises.

discussion questions 💬

1. Why did Elizabeth's baby leap within her?
2. Why did Mary sing a song of praise?

Instruments of Praise

what you need 🖌

- Small paper plates, two for each child
- Noise-maker materials (Dried beans, rice, etc.)
- Bowls, one for every two or three children
- Plastic spoons
- Crayons or markers
- Scissors
- Glue
- Stapler
- Children's Christmas worship CD and player

what you do ✂

Photocopy the music notes below, making at least two for each child. Place noise-maker materials in bowls and place on table where children will be working. Place several spoons next to the bowls. Make a sample instrument for children to use as reference and so that you can play along.

what children do 🖐

1. Color music notes and cut out. Younger children may want to cut the outside border, while older children cut out the note itself.
2. Glue music notes to a paper plate. Decorate paper plates with other drawings or designs.
3. Put one or two spoonfuls of noisemaker material in a plate.
4. Cover with a second plate and staple plates together around the rim.
5. As music plays, sing along and play noise-makers.

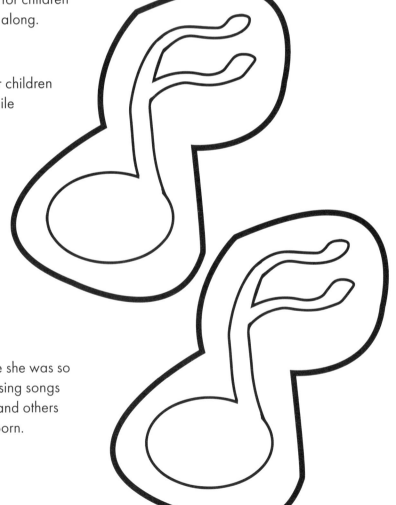

what to say 📣

Mary sang a song of praise to God because she was so happy that Jesus was going to be born. We sing songs of praise to God at Christmas to show God and others how happy we are that our Lord Jesus was born.

Verse Word Search

what you need ✎

- Pencils

what you do ✂

Before class, photocopy this page, making one for each child.

what children do ✋

Complete the word search by finding each word from the memory verse, "Oh, how my soul praises the Lord. How my spirit rejoices in God my Savior! (Luke 1:46–47). Don't forget to find *Luke*! Write each word on the appropriate blank line below. A word may appear more than once in the memory verse, but it will only appear once in the word search.

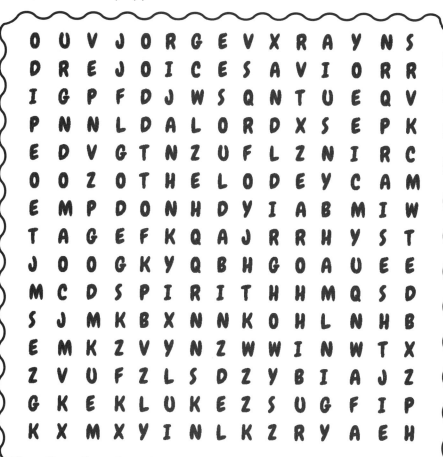

O U V J O R G E V X R A Y N S
D R E J O I C E S A V I O R R
I G P F D J W S Q N T U E Q V
P N N L D A L O R D X S E P K
E D V G T N Z U F L Z N I R C
O O Z O T H E L O D E Y C A M
E M P D O N H D Y I A B M I W
T A G E F K Q A J R R H Y S T
J O O G K Y Q B H G O A U E E
M C D S P I R I T H H M Q S D
S J M K B X N N K O H L N H B
E M K Z V Y N Z W W I N W T X
Z V U F Z L S D Z Y B I A J Z
G K E K L U K E Z S U G F I P
K X M X Y I N L K Z R Y A E H

" _____, ' _____ _____ _____ _____ _____ _____

_____. _____ _____ _____ _____ _____ _____

_____ _____ _____ _____!" _____ 1:46–47

Why Jesus Came Maze

what you need ✎
- Pencils

what you do ✂
Before class, photocopy this page, making one for each child.

what children do ✋
Find a path through the maze from heaven to Earth and write the letters on the blank lines at the bottom of the page. When you do, you'll read the reason God sent Jesus to be born on Earth. Elizabeth knew this before Mary could even say a word!

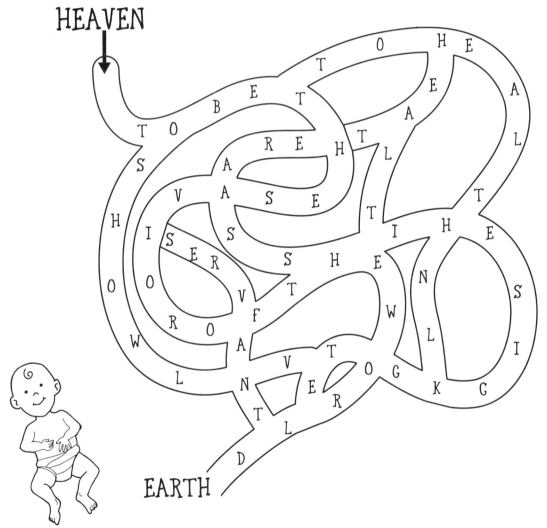

HEAVEN

EARTH

__ __ ___ ___ _____ __

___ _____ ___

Mary Visits Elizabeth

A Song of Praise (Based on Luke 1:39–56)

memory verse 📖

Oh, how my soul praises the Lord. How my spirit rejoices in God my Savior!
Luke 1:46–47

discussion questions 💬

1. Why did Elizabeth's baby leap within her?
2. Why did Mary sing a song of praise?

Family Fun Time Ideas

Go to Pillow Town

Grab your sofa cushions, bed pillows, blankets, afghans, and quilts. Throw them all on the floor of your living room and build a massive blanket fort for the whole family. Toss in everyone's favorite stuffed animals. Then, snuggle up together to read the story of Mary's visit to Elizabeth directly from the Bible. Follow it up with some snacks while watching Christmas classics on TV.

Decorate Your Home

As you work as a family, talk about family holiday traditions and what they mean to you.

- Deck your halls with boughs of holly. Fa-la-la-la-la, la-la, la, la.
- Make paper garlands, or origami ornaments to hang on the tree, over a door, or in the bedrooms.
- Decorate your windows with spray snow or stick-on decals.

Show Others God's Love

- As a family, purchase gifts for the charity your church is sponsoring.
- Take a few small gifts to a shelter for women and children.
- Raid the pantry—or better yet, purchase new canned goods to donate to a charity.
- Take homemade cookies and a card to your doctor's office, library, or church office.
- Secretly pay for the Santa photos of the family in line behind yours.
- Bake some doggie treats to take to an animal shelter.
- Wear Santa hats and go for a walk in your neighborhood. Bring garbage bags and sing Christmas carols as you pick up litter.

Jesus Is Born

memory verse

[Mary] gave birth to her firstborn son. She wrapped him snugly in strips of cloth and laid him in a manger.

Luke 2:7

Baby in A Manger
(Based on Luke 2:1–7)

When it was time for Jesus to be born, Mary and Joseph, had to make a long journey. They traveled from their home in Nazareth to Bethlehem to register for a census. It would have been scary to travel so far, but God had a plan.

Mary and Joseph finally arrived in Bethlehem. And they made it just in time—Jesus was on his way! Bethlehem was very busy because so many people were visiting for the census. Together, Mary and Joseph tried to find a place to stay. They tried inn after inn, but no one had room.

At last, one place took them in.

But there was only room for them to stay in the stable. It didn't seem like the place where a king would be born! But God knew what he was doing.

Mary safely gave birth to Jesus in the stable. She wrapped him in strips of cloth to keep him warm and laid him in a manger, where the animals ate. Jesus, our savior, entered the world as a humble baby in a manger.

discussion questions

1. Why was Jesus born in a stable?
2. Do you think Mary and Joseph were afraid? Why or why not?

Christmas Triptych

what you need 🖌

- Scissors
- Purple construction paper
- Crayons or markers
- Glue

what you do ✂

Before class, photocopy this page, making one for each child.

what children do ✋

1. Cut a sheet of purple construction paper in half lengthwise, then fold each half in thirds as shown, making one half for each child.
2. Color and cut out the pictures.
3. Glue pictures to the center of each matching pattern.
4. Glue one picture to each construction paper section.

what to say 📣

You can make a triptych, which is a three-fold picture. People made triptychs years ago for altars in beautiful churches. Put this in your room to remember Jesus' birth!

Luke 2:1-7

finished craft

Christmas Dial-a-scene

what you need ✏️

- White card stock
- Scissors
- Red construction paper
- Ruler
- Craft knife
- Crayons or markers
- Glue
- Hole punch
- Paper fasteners

what you do ✂️

Before class, photocopy this page onto white card stock, making one for each child. Cut a six-inch diameter circle of bright red construction paper for each child. Use a craft knife to cut a one-inch square window half an inch from the top of each circle and a thumb notch in the side, as shown.

what children do ✋

1. Color the dial-a-scene images.
2. Punch hole as indicated.
3. Place the red construction-paper cover over the circle and use a hole punch to make a hole in the same place as you did in the dial-a-scene sheet.
4. Attach the cover with a paper fastener.
5. Write "Christmas Dial-a-scene" and Luke 2:1–7 on the front.

what to say 📢

We made a dial that turns to show many Christmas scenes. You can show a friend the scenes as you turn the dial and tell the Christmas story.

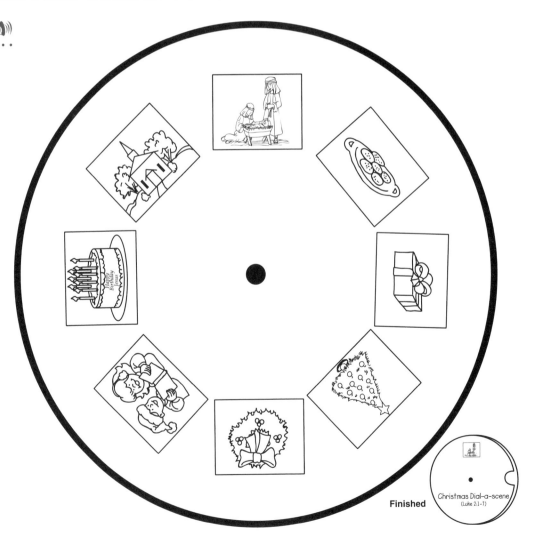

Finished

Christmas Dial-a-scene
(Luke 2:1–7)

Who, What, and Where?

what you need 🖌

- Bibles
- Crayons or markers

what you do ✂

Before class, photocopy this page, making one for each child.

what children do ✋

1. Read the names and places. Then read the descriptions on the other side of the page.
2. Write the correct number that goes with each person or place inside the star. Refer to Luke 2:1–7 in a Bible if you need help.

 1. Joseph

A. Animals' eating place

 2. Census

B. Place with no room that night

 3. Bethlehem

C. City where Joseph had to register

 4. Mary

D. Mary's first-born son

 5. Nazareth

E. Went to hometown to obey census law

 6. Manger

F. Chosen by God to be Jesus' mother

 7. Inn

G. Where Mary and Joseph lived

 8. Jesus

H. Reason Mary and Joseph had to travel

Jesus Is Born

Baby in A Manger (Based on Luke 2:1–7)

memory verse 📖

[Mary] gave birth to her firstborn son. She wrapped him snugly in strips of cloth and laid him in a manger.
Luke 2:7

discussion questions 💬

1. Why was Jesus born in a stable?
2. Do you think Mary and Joseph were afraid? Why or why not?

Stained Glass Window

God's Son might have been born in a palace to royal parents. Instead, Jesus arrived in a place where animals slept and ate. He slept in a manger, where cows kept their food. He was raised by Mary and Joseph, who were ordinary people. God planned Jesus' humble birth.

1. Color the stained glass window using bright colors.
2. Trace over the lines with a black marker.
3. Cut out the image and glue onto black construction paper.

The Shepherds' Surprise

memory verse 📖

Glory to God in highest heaven, and peace on earth to those with whom God is pleased.
Luke 2:14

Shepherd's Share the Good News
(Based on Luke 2:8–20)

The same night that Jesus was born, some shepherds were working in a nearby field and became the first to know about the good news. The shepherds were guarding their flock when a bright light suddenly filled the sky. It was an angel!

At first, the shepherds were afraid, but the angel said he brought good news. Their savior, Jesus, had just been born right there in Bethlehem! The angel told the shepherds how to recognize their Savior: they would

find a baby wrapped in strips of cloth, lying in a manger.

Imagine how the shepherds must have felt after hearing this! Before they could think, though, thousands of other angels joined the first angel. They sang, "Glory to God in highest heaven, and peace on earth to those with whom God is pleased."

The shepherds ran to Bethlehem and found baby Jesus, Joseph, and Mary. They were so excited about what happened, so they rushed to tell everyone the good news that the Savior had come.

discussion questions 💬

1. What did the angels tell the shepherds?
2. Why do you think shepherds were the first to hear about Jesus' birth?

Racing Shepherd

what you need ✎

- Scissors
- Yarn
- Yardstick
- Cardboard
- Crayons or markers
- Hole punch

what you do ✂

Before class, photocopy this page, making one for each child. Cut yarn into nine-foot pieces. Cut out three-by-seven-inch squares of cardboard.

what children do 🖐

1. Color and cut out the shepherd.
2. Glue the shepherd to a piece of cardboard.
3. Punch a hole in the center where indicated.
4. Thread yarn through the hole and tie a knot on either end.
5. Have a race: partner up with one person holding each end of yarn. Wiggle the yarn to move the shepherd up and down.

Luke 2:8-20

Hidden Shepherd Story

what you need ✐
- Crayons or markers

what you do ✂
Before class, photocopy this page, making one for each child.

what children do 🖐
1. Read the word list and search for the words in the puzzle.
2. Circle each word in the puzzle as you go.

SHEPHERDS	ANGEL	CHRIST	LORD
FIELDS	JOY	BABY	MARY
FLOCK	NEWS	MANGER	JOSEPH
NIGHT	SAVIOR	PEACE	

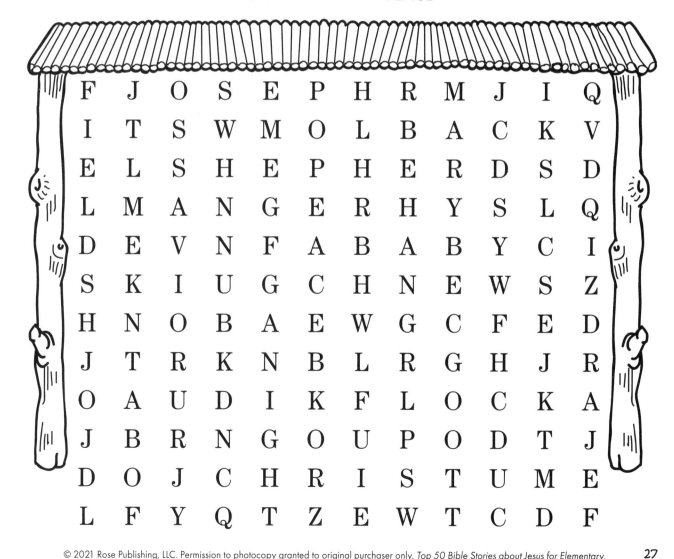

```
F J O S E P H R M J I Q
I T S W M O L B A C K V
E L S H E P H E R D S D
L M A N G E R H Y S L Q
D E V N F A B A B Y C I
S K I U G C H N E W S Z
H N O B A E W G C F E D
J T R K N B L R G H J R
O A U D I K F L O C K A
J B R N G O U P O D T J
D O J C H R I S T U M E
L F Y Q T Z E W T C D F
```

Angel and Shepherd Banner

what you need 🖌

- Colored paper
- Crayons or markers
- Scissors
- Glue
- Tabloid sized paper, one per child
- Hole punch
- Yarn

what you do ✂

Before class, photocopy this page onto colored paper, making one for each child.

what children do ✋

1. Cut apart and decorate the figures.
2. Glue figures onto the tabloid sized paper. This will be the banner.
3. Punch holes into the top corners of the banner.
4. Thread yarn through both holes and secure at the ends.

finished craft

The Shepherds' Surprise

Shepherd's Share the Good News (Based on Luke 2:8–20)

memory verse 📖

Glory to God in highest heaven, and peace on earth to those with whom God is pleased.
Luke 2:14

discussion questions 💬

1. What did the angels tell the shepherds?
2. Why do you think shepherds were the first to hear about Jesus' birth?

Shepherd Story Path

Color the path and the pictures along the path. Then, use the path and the numbered story to share the good news of Jesus' birth with a friend or family member.

1. The shepherds sat guarding their sheep.
2. A bright light lit up the darkness, and an angel told them God's Son had been born. More angels sang "Glory to God in the highest."
3. The shepherds hurried away to find Jesus.
4. They found Jesus. The angel was right!
5. The shepherds saw Jesus wrapped in swaddling clothes, lying in a manger.
6. The shepherds left, telling the Good News and praising God everywhere they went.

Wise Men Look for Jesus

memory verse 📖

Those who search will surely find me.
Proverbs 8:17

Following a Star (based on Matthew 2:1–11)

Shortly after Jesus was born, some special visitors came to Bethlehem to worship him. Wise men from the East, also known as Magi, had been watching and waiting for signs from God that the Savior would come. They followed a sign of a star to where Jesus was born.

First, the wise men visited King Herod. They asked, "Where is the newborn king? We want to worship him." This made King Herod jealous. King Herod told the wise men to go to Bethlehem, find baby Jesus, and come back to tell him where to find him.

The wise men continued to follow the star to Bethlehem. When they found Jesus and his family, they bowed down and worshiped him. Then, they gave him gifts fit for a king: gold, frankincense, and myrrh. When it was time to leave, the wise men didn't return to King Herod. Instead, God warned them to return home a different way. So baby Jesus was safe with his family, all according to God's plan.

discussion questions 💬

1. Who were the wise men and what did they do?
2. Why did King Herod want to know where Jesus was?

Coded Message

what you need ✎

- Crayons or markers

what you do ✂

Before class, photocopy this page, making one for each child.

what children do ✋

1. Follow the key to uncover this coded message. The letters above the blanks refer to the bold letter in the key. On the blank lines, write the letter found under the bold letter.

what to say 📣

The wise men followed a coded message. They knew that the special star meant that God's Son had been born. By following the star, the wise men were able to find the exact place where God's Son lay. Just as God guided them to baby Jesus, God will guide us to Jesus when we look for him.

Code Key

A	B	C	D	E	F	G	H	I	J	K	L	M
Z	Y	X	W	V	U	T	S	R	Q	P	O	N

Z	Y	X	W	V	U	T	S	R	Q	P	O	N
A	B	C	D	E	F	G	H	I	J	K	L	M

1. From where did the wise men travel?

G S V   V Z H G

— — —   — — — —

2. Who was king at this time?

S V I L W

— — — —

3. Who had the prophets promised would come out of Bethlehem?

Z   T L E V I M L I

—   — — — — — — — —

4. In which land was Bethlehem located?

Q F W Z S

— — — — —

5. How did the wise men find Jesus?

Z   H G Z I

—   — — — —

6. What did the wise men do when they found Jesus?

U V O O   W L D M   &
— — — —   — — — —   &

D L I H S R K K V W

— — — — — — — — —

7. What did the wise men open to give Jesus gifts?

G I V Z H F I V H

— — — — — — — — —

8. How were the wise men warned about Herod's wicked plans?

Z   W I V Z N

—   — — — — —

9. How did they go home without Herod catching them?

Z M L G S V I   D Z B

— — — — — — —   — — —

Star Ornament

what you need ✎

- Thin cardboard or cardstock
- Craft knife
- Table covering
- Construction paper
- Scissors
- Crayons or markers
- Hole punch
- Yarn
- Glue
- Glitter

what you do ✂

Before class, photocopy this page, making one for each child. Use the pattern to cut stars from cardboard or card stock, one for every two or three children. Place a table covering on tables.

what children do ✋

1. Use a thin cardboard or card stock star to trace a star on construction paper and cut it out.
2. Glue it to the cardboard star.
3. Punch a hole in the top.
4. String 6-inch yarn through hole and tie ends in a knot to make a hanger.
5. Use glue to create a design on the star. You can flood the whole star with glue, or draw swirls, dots, or other patterns.
6. Pour glitter on the glue and allow to dry, shaking off excess glitter.

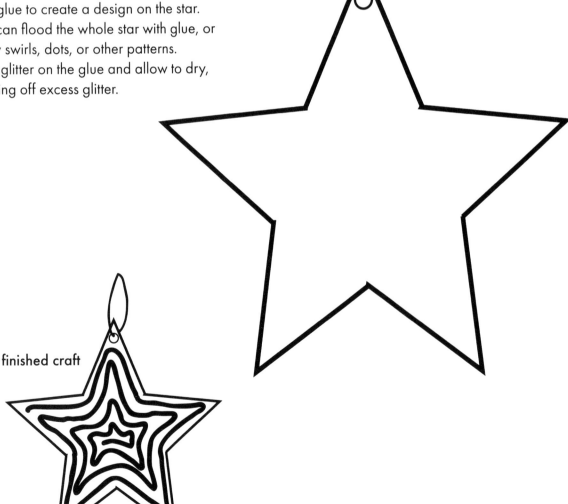

finished craft

Wise Men Quiz

what you need

- Bibles
- Crayons or markers

what you do ✂

Before class, photocopy this page, making one for each child. Read Matthew 2:1–11 aloud and review the Bible story.

what children do ✋

1. Read the statements below.
2. If you think the sentence is correct, print YES. If you think the sentence is wrong, print NO.

what to say 📣

You will find that some parts of the story of the wise men below have been changed. See how much you know about what really happened.

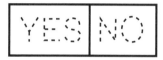 **1.** The wise men saw a cloud in the sky and followed it.

 **2.** The wise men went to Jerusalem to find the King of the Jews.

 **3.** The wise men stopped at a hotel to look for Jesus.

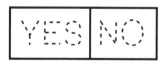 **4.** Bad King Herod pretended to be happy about Jesus' birth.

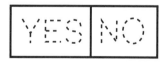 **5.** The wise men found Jesus and gave him a bath.

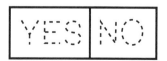 **6.** The wise men told King Herod where to find Jesus.

Wise Men Look for Jesus

Following a Star (based on Matthew 2:1–11)

memory verse 📖

Those who search will surely find me.
Proverbs 8:17

discussion questions 💬

1. Who were the wise men and what did they do?
2. Why did King Herod want to know where Jesus was?

Wise Men's Trail Mix Gift

You can make some Wise Men's Trail Mix, as they perhaps carried with them on their journey. Make it as a gift to share with a friend. Tell your friend about the wise men and how they looked for Jesus and found him.

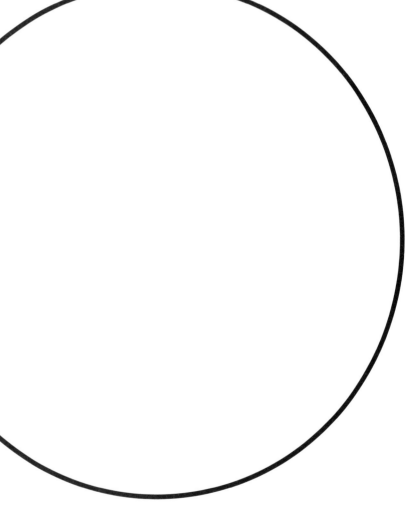

1. Mix one cup each of raisins, pretzel sticks, cereal pieces, peanuts, and chocolate bits.
2. Divide trail mix into small, resealable plastic bags.
3. Use the pattern to cut a circle from red construction paper, one for each bag.
4. Write the memory verse on the circle. Decorate the rest of the circle.
5. Tape one circle to the front of each bag.
6. Share the trail mix with friends or family members.

Simeon & Anna See Jesus

memory verse 📖

I will praise you, LORD, with all my heart.
Psalm 9:1

Seeing the Savior (based on Luke 2:22–38)

When Jesus was little, his parents took him to Jerusalem so they could dedicate him to God at the temple. This was one of the laws they followed as Jews.

Many people lived in Jerusalem, including many people who loved God. One of those people was a man named Simeon. God told Simeon that he would live to see the Messiah, or Jesus. When Mary and Joseph presented Jesus at the temple, Simeon was there! He was so excited to see baby Jesus that he began praising God. He said that Jesus would be a savior. Mary and Joseph were amazed that this man knew Jesus.

Anna, a woman who also loved God, was also at the temple at this time. When she heard what Simeon was saying about baby Jesus, she began praising God, too! They were so excited to see their Savior. After seeing Jesus, Anna told everyone she knew that the Savior they had been waiting for had come.

discussion questions 💬

1. Who did Jesus, Mary, and Joseph meet in Jerusalem?
2. Why were Anna and Simeon excited to see Jesus?

A Row of Friends

what you need ✐

- Scissors
- Crayons or markers

what you do ✂

Before class, photocopy this page, making one for each child.

what children do 🖐

1. Cut out the rectangle on the solid black lines.
2. Fold the paper on the dashed lines accordion-style.
3. Cut along the solid line through all thicknesses.
4. When you unfold the figures, think of some friends you want to tell about Jesus.
5. Write a name on each of the figures and decorate them.
6. Stand it up to remind you to tell others about Jesus.

what to say 📢

Anna was so excited about seeing Jesus that she went to all of her friends and told them the Messiah was born. Do you have some friends you could tell about Jesus?

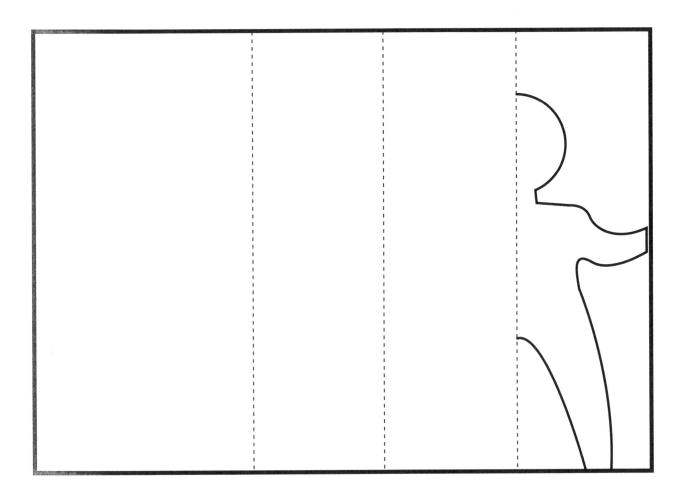

Figure it Out

what you need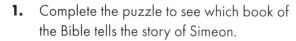

- Crayons or markers

what you do ✂

Before class, photocopy this page, making one for each child.

what children do 🖐

1. Complete the puzzle to see which book of the Bible tells the story of Simeon.

A letter in LAKE but not in BAKE. _____

A letter in USE, UNCLE and UNICORN. _____

A letter in TAKE but not in TALE. _____

A letter in BITE, BYE and FEAR. _____

Do you know what this man's occupation was?
Hint: Today he would work in a hospital and wear a stethoscope around his neck.

_____

This man included Simeon's prayer in his gospel. Read Luke 2:30–32 (NLT) and fill in the blanks of the prayer.

"I have seen your _____, which you have prepared for all

_____. He is a light to reveal _____ to

the nations and he is the _____ of your people Israel!"

A Silly Story

what you need ✏

- Paper

what you do ✂

Before class, photocopy this page, making one for each child. During class, read the story below to the children. Then, read it again, asking the children to stand when a silly word is said. Choose a child to correct the silly word with the correct word from the Word Box. Choose a volunteer to read the line after it is corrected.

what to say 📢

Listen to this story. Is it silly? When you hear a silly word that doesn't belong, stand up. If you're standing, I'll ask you to pick a word from the word box to correct the story.

Word Box

Amazed	Seen	Temple	Died
Jesus	Simeon	Dedicated	Arms

Mary and Joseph brought Jesus to the theater so he could be eaten. While they were there they saw a man named Craig. Simeon had been waiting to see the Messiah before he ate. The Holy Spirit had revealed to Simeon that he would not die until he saw monkeys. When Simeon saw Jesus, he took the baby in his car, praising God. He said, "I am content. I have lost the Messiah as you promised." Joseph and Mary were sad at the things Simeon said to them.

Simeon & Anna See Jesus

Seeing the Savior (based on Luke 2:22–38)

memory verse 📖

I will praise you, LORD, with all my heart.
Psalm 9:1

discussion questions 💬

1. Who did Jesus, Mary, and Joseph meet in Jerusalem?
2. Why were Anna and Simeon excited to see Jesus?

Sharing Jesus Letter

When Anna saw Jesus, she could not keep quiet. She told everyone who had been looking for the coming of the Savior that he had arrived.

What about you? Have you told anyone about Jesus? In the thought balloon below, write the names of some friends you could tell about Jesus. Then write a letter to share your knowledge of Jesus. Explain that Jesus wants to be your friends' Savior, too.

Jesus Grows Up

memory verse 📖

Jesus grew in wisdom and in stature and in favor with God and all the people.
Luke 2:52

In My Father's House (based on Luke 2:41–52)

Jesus and his parents visited the temple every year to celebrate Passover. The family traveled in large groups of other families from Nazareth to the big city of Jerusalem.

Something surprising happened on this trip when Jesus was twelve years old. When the celebration in the city was over, everyone headed home. Mary and Joseph didn't see Jesus with them, but they weren't worried at first because they thought he was with the other travelers. They started to worry, though, when he didn't come home that night.

Mary and Joseph returned to Jerusalem to look for Jesus. Where could he be? Finally, they stopped by the temple. And there was Jesus! He was sitting with the religious teachers, listening, teaching, and asking questions. Everyone was amazed at what he had to say.

At first, his parents were upset. "Why did you leave us?" they asked. But Jesus replied, "I was in my Father's house." Mary and Joseph didn't know what he meant. Jesus was saying that he is God's son—and he is!

Jesus returned to Nazareth with his parents, and he was always obedient. There, he grew up, becoming a wise and loving young man.

discussion questions 💬

1. Why did Jesus and his family visit Jerusalem?
2. What did Jesus mean when he said he was in his Father's house?

What Would Jesus Do?

what you need 🖌

• Scissors
• Glue

what you do ✂

Before class, photocopy this page, making one for each child. Read through the questions or ask for volunteers to read. Discuss the situations one at a time.

what children do ✋

1. Cut out each YES and NO box.
2. For each number, ask: would Jesus have done this? If so, glue YES in the box. If not, glue NO in the box.

what to say 📢

Sometimes we only think of Jesus as grown up, but he was once a child, just like you. Jesus made decisions whether or not to obey his parents and God, just like you do. But since he never sinned, he always obeyed. What would that look like for the choices you have to make?

	1. Brian's mom wasn't feeling well. He watched his baby sister so his mom could rest.
	2. The new family next door to Jay was lonely. Jay invited them to her church.
	3. Abby received too much change at the store. She kept it.
	4. Luke made breakfast for his little sister so his parents could sleep later.
	5. When Jason fell on the playground, Lauren laughed and ran away.
	6. Chris raked the leaves when his father asked him to.
	7. When David's family bought a new car, Griffin threw a rock at it.
	8. Cassie helped her grandmother do chores before going to the park to play.
	9. Kyle took extra cookies at school when no one was looking.
	10. Jon gave one of his favorite games to a Christmas toy drive for needy children.

YES	YES	YES	NO	NO
YES	YES	YES	NO	NO

Growing Four Ways

what you need ✎

- Crayons or markers

what you do ✂

Before class, photocopy this page, making one for each child.

what children do ✋

1. Color each of the four boxes on the right a different color.
2. Read each sentence below. Decide whether the sentence is growing in wisdom, stature, favor with others, or favor with God.
3. Draw a line from the sentence to the appropriate box using its matching color.

what to say 📢

As the years went by, Jesus grew in four different ways. Jesus grew wiser. He grew taller. He grew in his relationships with others. And he grew in his closeness to God. You and your friends are growing in many of these same ways.

1. Logan can reach the tools on the top of the work bench without a stool. •

2. Lauren does her homework each day before calling her friends. •

3. Griffin has outgrown last year's jacket. •

4. James invited Kyle to a ball game. •

5. Amber loves to read her Bible each day. •

6. Joshua gives part of his allowance to church. •

7. Natalie eats healthy snacks. •

8. Jessica can run faster and farther than last year. •

9. Payton talks to God about his problems. •

10. Tim obeys all traffic laws when he rides his bicycle. •

11. Lilly keeps secrets shared with her. •

12. John asks God for patience with a mean classmate. •

| GROWING IN WISDOM |

| GROWING IN STATURE (Height) |

| GROWING IN FAVOR WITH OTHERS |

| GROWING IN FAVOR WITH GOD |

Temple Story Completion

what you need ✎

- Crayons or markers

what you do ✂

Before class, photocopy this page, making one for each child. Review the story. After they fill in the blanks, review the answers. Talk about any that seemed to be confusing.

what children do ✋

1. Read the words written beside the scrolls below.
2. Then read the story and choose the best word from the list below to complete the sentences.
3. Write the correct word or number in each space to complete the story.

what to say 📢

Jesus went to the temple to worship God, just as we go to church. He showed us that going to church is important. He also showed us that church is a place where we can listen to and learn about God.

Jesus went to (a)_____ with Mary and Joseph.
They were going to celebrate (b)_____.
After celebrating, Mary and Joseph found Jesus in the
(c)_____. He was (d)_____
to the teachers and (e)_____ them
(f)_____. All who heard Jesus were
(g)_____ at his (h)_____ and
his (i)_____. Jesus said that he must be about
his (j)_____ (k)_____.

1	answers	7	understanding
2	astonished	8	Father's
3	Jerusalem	9	questions
4	listening	10	temple
5	business	11	asking
6	Passover		

Jesus Grows Up

In My Father's House (based on Luke 2:41–52)

memory verse 📖

Jesus grew in wisdom and in stature and in favor with God and all the people.
Luke 2:52

discussion questions 💬

1. Why did Jesus and his family visit Jerusalem?
2. What did Jesus mean when he said he was in his Father's house?

Make and Bake Hand Print

As Jesus grew older, he grew bigger, just as you are growing. Someday your hand will be much bigger than it is now. You can make a print of your hand in baking clay to help you remember that you are growing, just as Jesus grew. You'll need an adult to help with this recipe. This recipe makes enough for four hand prints, so ask a friend or family member to help you.

1. Mix 4 cups of flour and 1 cup of salt with ½ cup of hot water.
2. Knead for 6 to 8 minutes. Add more flour if the dough is too sticky.
3. Divide the dough into four parts.
4. Use this template to cut a 6-inch aluminum foil circle for each hand print.
5. Place a dollop of dough on each piece of foil and press a hand into the dough to make a print.
6. Poke a hole near the top with a pencil for hanging.
7. Bake at 350°F for one hour or longer.
8. Paint the prints with tempera paint.
9. Once dry, thread and knot yarn through the hole to make a hanger.

finished craft

Section 2
Jesus' Life & Ministry

Jesus Is Baptized

memory verse 📖

Anyone who believes and is baptized will be saved.
Mark 16:16

Baptized by Cousin John (based on Matthew 3:11–17)

Jesus had a cousin named John. John preached to others that the Messiah, or Jesus, was coming. When people believed his message, John baptized them as a sign of their new life in Jesus. Some people called him John the Baptist.

One day, Jesus asked John to baptize him. At first, John was surprised. Jesus was the Messiah! "I am the one who needs to be baptized by you," John said, "so why are you coming to me?" But Jesus said it had to be done. It was part of God's plan.

So John baptized Jesus. When Jesus came up out of the water, the Bible says that the Spirit of God descended on him like a dove. Then, God said, "This is my dearly loved Son, who brings me great joy." Even today, Christians are baptized to show that God has given them a new life. It's part of following Jesus' example and God's plan.

discussion questions 💬
1. Who was John the Baptist?
2. Why did John baptize Jesus?

Just Like Jesus

what you need ✎

- Scissors
- Crayons or markers

what you do ✂

Before class, photocopy this page, making one for each child. If children have trouble thinking of a word for one of the letters, give some suggestions. (J: joyful; E: example; S: sympathetic; U: unselfish; S: steadfast.)

what children do ✋

1. Cut out the image below.
2. Color the image.
3. On the lines beside JESUS, write a characteristic of Jesus that you want to be like.

I Want To Be Like

J _____
E _____
S _____
U _____
S _____

Whoooo? Whoooo?

what you need

- Bibles
- Crayons or markers

what you do ✂

Before class, photocopy this page, making one for each child.

what children do ✋

1. Complete the code.
2. Look up Luke 1:5 and Luke 2:16 to check your answers.

what to say 📣

The wise old owl below thinks he is pretty smart, but there are some things that stump him. He knows that John the Baptist was Jesus' cousin, and that means John's parents would be Jesus' aunt and uncle. What he doesn't know are the aunt's and uncle's names. Using the code can you figure them out? Hint: A=1 and B=2.

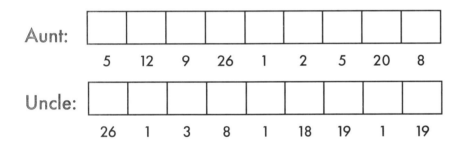

Aunt:

5	12	9	26	1	2	5	20	8

Uncle:

26	1	3	8	1	18	19	1	19

Now that you've straightened out the owl on that puzzle, he wants to know the names of John's aunt and uncle.

Aunt:

13	1	18	25

Uncle:

10	15	19	5	16	8

Whooooose parents are they? _____.

Where's the Word?

what you need ✎
- Pencils

what you do ✂
Before class, photocopy this page, making one for each child.

what children do ✋
John the Baptist was surprised when Jesus asked him to perform his baptism. John knew that Jesus was God's Son. Jesus was baptized to set an example for us. Getting baptized is a way to show that we love and follow Jesus.

In the word search below, circle all of the words from the word box. These are words from today's Bible story about the baptism of Jesus.

Word Box

GALILEE	JORDAN	SPIRIT	LOVE	WATER
HEAVEN	JESUS	JOHN	FULFILL	LIGHT
VOICE	BAPTIZED	DESCENDING	DOVE	PLEASED

```
C S P I R I T E G F P L F Z D
F G B U P W C L A B V X D U E
F A O I K A E G A X A O L T S
U P B A P T I Z E D D O V E C
L Q F R U E Q D M I K H H W E
F K B I I R V O I C E E Z J N
I P K M J Z U P M R I A B O D
L L I G H T O L V N E V G S I
L A G A L I L E E J F E Q H N
R U E E V Q H A U O R N B Y G
T K C J F G L S L R C I F T Z
Z E S G N C L E E D N L Z V G
J K N C P V P D V A M M M G Y
R H Z X Q P S D P N G U B R T
J O H N B L O V E P J E S U S
```

Jesus Is Baptized

Baptized by Cousin John (based on Matthew 3:11–17)

memory verse 📖

Anyone who believes and is baptized will be saved.
Mark 16:16

discussion questions 💬

1. Who was John the Baptist?
2. Why did John baptize Jesus?

Color Coded

Color the picture below according to the color code.
Then draw and color the sun.

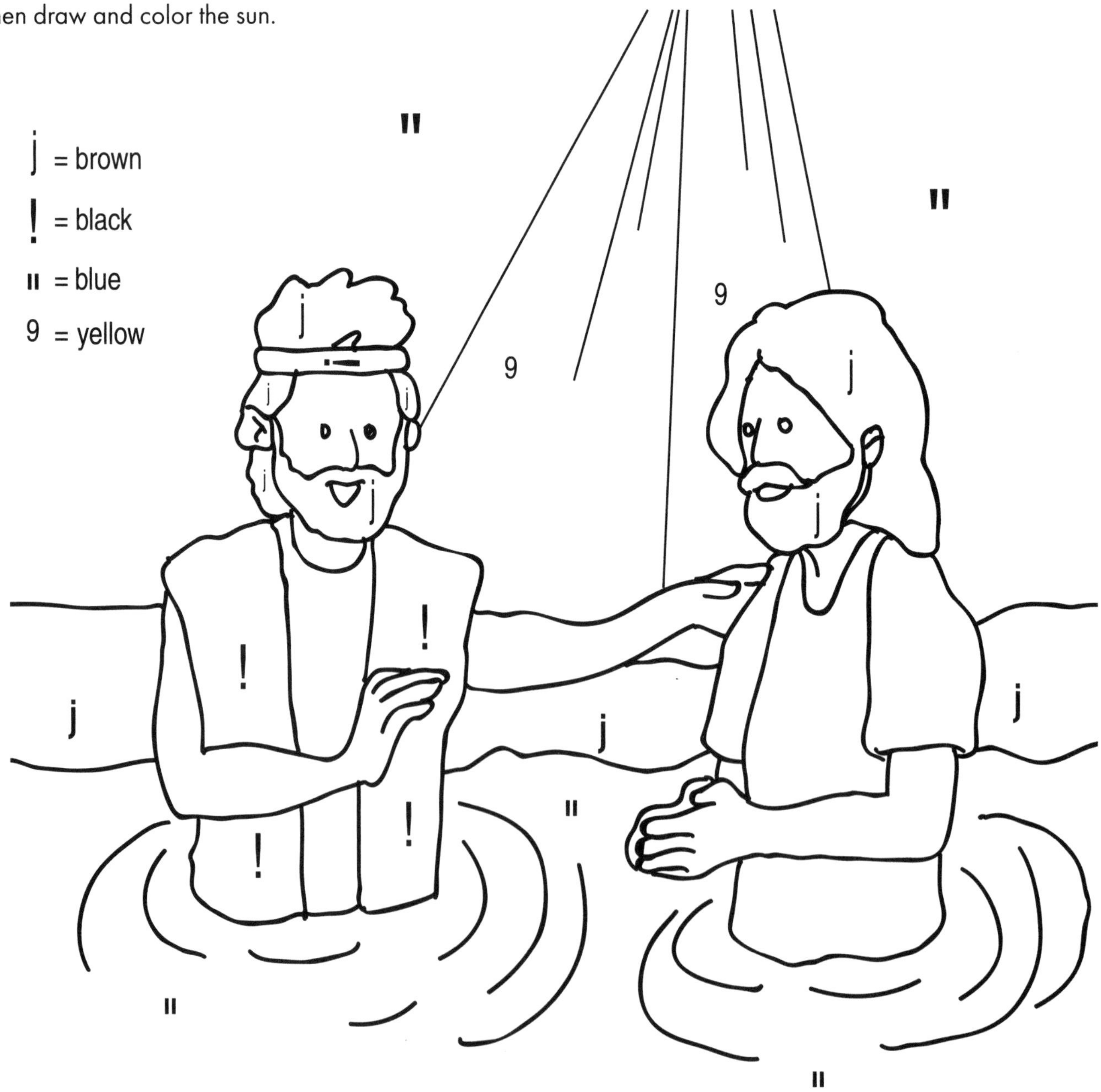

j = brown

! = black

ıı = blue

9 = yellow

Jesus Is Tempted

memory verse

You must worship the LORD your God and serve only him.
Matthew 4:10

Say No to Satan (based on Matthew 4:1–11)

Jesus was perfect, so he never sinned. But he was still human, so he faced the same problems that we face. In fact, Satan tried to tempt Jesus to sin several times. What do you think Jesus did?

One time, Jesus went to the wilderness to fast and pray. He went forty days and forty nights without eating. He must have been very hungry and feeling weak.

Knowing that Jesus would be feeling weak, Satan came to him and tried to tempt him. First, Satan said, "If you are the Son of God, tell these stones to become loaves of bread." Satan wanted Jesus to make his own food instead of relying on God. But Jesus said no, he would rely only on God.

Next, Satan took Jesus to the top of the temple. There, he told Jesus to jump off the ledge, saying the angels would protect him. But again, Jesus said no, he would not test God.

Finally, Satan showed Jesus all the kingdoms of the world. "I will give it all to you," Satan said, "if you will kneel down and worship me."

How do you think Jesus responded? He said "Get out of here, Satan." He said he would only worship God. After that, the devil finally went away, and the Bible says the angels came to take care of him.

We might find ourselves in situations like Jesus was in, where Satan tempts us to sin. But we don't have to sin. We can say, "Get out of here, Satan," and rely on God to take care of us.

discussion

questions

1. Why was Jesus in the wilderness?
2. What was the last thing Jesus said to Satan? Why did he say that?

What Did Satan Do?

what you need ✐

- Bibles
- Crayons or markers

what you do ✂

Before class, photocopy this page, making one for each child.

what children do ✋

1. Think back to the Bible story. Then, read the statements below.
2. Find the three ways Satan tempted Jesus that day in the wilderness. Draw a heart in the box of each correct answer.
3. Put an *X* in the boxes that are incorrect.
4. Look up Matthew 4:1–11 if you need help.

what to say 📢

When you're tempted to sin, remember that you're not alone. God will help you do the right thing when you are tempted to do something wrong.

1. Satan tempted Jesus to turn the water into soda pop.

2. Satan tempted Jesus to turn the rocks into bread.

3. Satan tempted Jesus to jump down from the temple's roof.

4. Satan tempted Jesus to jump out of an airplane.

5. Satan tempted Jesus to mow the grass on the mountain.

6. Satan tempted Jesus to bow down to him.

Bonus Question: Who took care of Jesus when Satan left him alone?

_____

Sword of the Spirit

what you need ✏️

- Bibles
- Scissors
- Crayons or markers
- Glue
- Foil

what you do ✂️

Before class, photocopy this page, making one for each child. Cut out sections of foil to wrap around the blade of the sword, one for each child.

what children do ✋

1. Cut out the sword.
2. Decorate the sword's handle.
3. Place glue on one side of the blade.
4. Center the foil over the blade and press onto the glue.
5. Turn the sword over and place glue on the backside.
6. Wrap the foil over the back, folding in as the blade narrows.
7. After it dries, use the sword to mark Matthew 4:10 in your Bible.

what to say 📢

Jesus used a special weapon to defeat Satan. It is a weapon we can use today. That weapon is God's Word. In Ephesians 6:17, the Bible is called "the sword of the Spirit." Read and memorize God's Word daily so that when Satan comes to tempt you, your sword will be ready to defeat him.

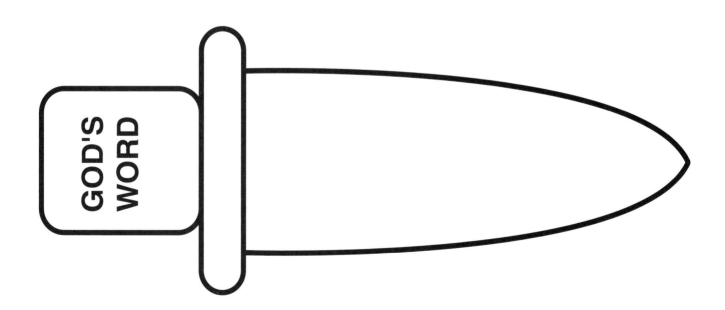

GOD'S WORD

Temptation Word Search

what you need ✏

- Crayons or markers

what you do ✂

Before class, photocopy this page, making one for each child.

what children do ✋

1. Find all the words in the word box.
2. Write the leftover letters on the line and see what they tell you to say when you are tempted.

what to say 📢

Can we be tempted, even after we ask Jesus into our lives? Jesus was tempted, and he had never sinned. Even after we have Jesus in our lives, we are still tempted to do wrong things. But when we are tempted, we can ask Jesus to help us stay away from what tempts us.

JESUS	FORTY
SATAN	TEMPT

```
F  O  R  T  Y
J  G  T  O  A
E  W  E  A  Y
S  S  M  A  T
U  A  P  N  !
S  A  T  A  N
```

___ ___ ___   ___ ___ ___ ___ ___

___ ___ ___ ___ ___ ___ ___

Jesus Is Tempted

Say No to Satan (based on Matthew 4:1–11)

memory verse 📖

You must worship the LORD your God and serve only him.
Matthew 4:10

discussion questions 💬

1. Why was Jesus in the wilderness?
2. What was the last thing Jesus said to Satan? Why did he say that?

finished craft

Laziness
Those unwilling to
work will not get
to eat.
2 Thessalonians 3:10

God's Word Says

Jesus used the Word of God to defeat Satan. That's why it's good to memorize Bible verses. They can help us defeat Satan.

1. Write each verse on a colored index card.
2. Decorate the cards.
3. Punch a hole in the top left corner of each card.
4. Thread a keyring through the holes to keep the cards together.
5. When you are tempted to lie, repeat the verse on honesty. If you are tempted to take something that doesn't belong to you, repeat the verse on stealing.

Honesty: *Stop telling lies. Let us tell our neighbors the truth.* Ephesians 4:25

Stealing: *If you are a thief, quit stealing. Instead, use your hands for good hard work, and then give generously to others in need.* Ephesians 4:28

Laziness: *Those unwilling to work will not get to eat.* 2 Thessalonians 3:10

Selfishness: *Don't look out only for your own interests, but take an interest in others, too.* Philippians 2:4

Envy: *Don't love money; be satisfied with what you have.* Hebrews 13:5

Gossiping: *The wicked are trapped by their own words, but the godly escape such trouble.* Proverbs 12:13

Quarreling: *A servant of the Lord must not quarrel but must be kind to everyone.* 2 Timothy 2:24

Unforgiveness: *Be kind to each other, tenderhearted, forgiving one another, just as God through Christ has forgiven you.* Ephesians 4:32

Disobedience: *Listen when your father corrects you. Don't neglect your mother's instruction.* Proverbs 1:8

Nets Full of Fish

memory verse 📖

A real friend sticks closer than a brother.
Proverbs 18:24

Cast Your Nets (based on Luke 5:1–11)

One day, Jesus was preaching by the Sea of Galilee. Many people came to hear what he had to say. While he was preaching, Jesus noticed the fishermen and their boats on the shore. They were washing their nets after fishing all night.

Jesus walked up to a boat that belonged to a man named Simon Peter. Jesus asked Simon Peter if he could use his boat so he could preach to the crowds from the water.

When he finished preaching, Jesus asked Simon Peter to take the boat out deeper and to let the nets out to catch fish.

"Master," Simon replied, "we worked hard all last night and didn't catch a thing. But if you say so, I'll let the nets down again."

Simon Peter didn't think they would catch many fish. But when they brought the nets up, they were filled with fish! There were too many for them to take in! Simon Peter called to his friends, James and John, to help, and together they filled two boats with fish.

Simon Peter and his friends were amazed. But Jesus said, "Don't be afraid! From now on you'll be fishing for people!" He wanted them to follow him and be his disciples! And Simon Peter, James, and John did just that. They gave up everything they had and followed Jesus. They were his first disciples.

discussion questions 💬

1. Why did people gather around Jesus?
2. What did Jesus tell the men when he asked them to be his disciples?

A Colorful School of Fish

what you need ✏

- Tissue paper, multiple colors
- Scissors
- Spray bottle
- Water
- Trash can
- Hole punch
- Fishing wire
- Tape

what you do ✂

Before class, photocopy this page, making one for each child. Tear tissue paper into small pieces. Distribute pieces of colorful tissue paper.

what children do ✋

1. Cut out the fish.
2. Spritz water on the fish.
3. Arrange the pieces of tissue paper on top.
4. When covered, spritz the paper again and allow to dry.
5. Carefully lift the tissue papers off the fish and throw them away. The tissue-paper color will remain on the fish.
6. Punch a hole where indicated.
7. Tie fishing wire through the hole and hang the fish from the ceiling with tape.

← hole

A Fishy Tale

what you need ✏

- Scissors
- Crayons or markers

what you do ✂

Before class, photocopy this page, making one for each child.

what children do ✋

1. Color and cut out the fish.
2. Put them in the correct order based on the story.

Mend the Net

what you need 🖊
- Crayons or markers

what you do ✂
Before class, photocopy this page, making one for each child.

what children do ✋
1. Read the poem below.
2. Some of the lines have missing words. Can you figure out the rhyming words that are missing?
3. Fill in the blank with the correct rhyming word. Hint: the missing word rhymes with the line that comes before. The first part of each word is filled in for you.

Peter and Andrew were mending their nets.

It was one of those nights they wanted to **forg** _____ .

Although they fished and fished all night,

There still wasn't one little fish in **s** _____.

"Go back out," the Son of God said,

"Now those fish are out of **b** _____."

Down went the nets — down, down, down.

Up came the nets, and look what they **f** _____!

Their nets were full and starting to break.

It's a good thing friends were on the **l** _____.

The fishermen looked at each other with a nod.

Now they knew Jesus was the Son of **G** _____.

Nets Full of Fish

Cast Your Nets (based on Luke 5:1–11)

memory verse 📖

A real friend sticks closer than a brother.

Proverbs 18:24

discussion questions 💬

1. Why did people gather around Jesus?
2. What did Jesus tell the men when he asked them to be his disciples?

Mend the Net

1. Choose a partner to play the game with you. Decide who will go first.
2. The first player will connect two dots, then the second player will do the same.
3. If you make a box on your turn, print your initial in the square. The goal is to see how many squares you can make with your initial in them.
4. When you are done, the net should be mended!

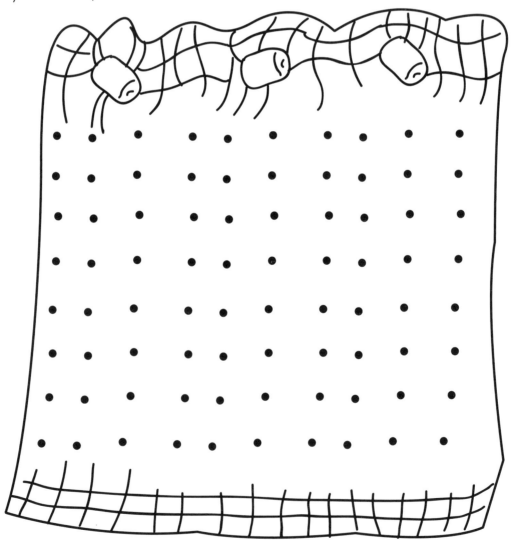

Jesus' Friends

memory verse 📖

Jesus called out to them, "Come, follow me, and I will show you how to fish for people!"
Matthew 4:19

Follow Me (based on Matthew 4:18–22; Luke 5:27–28)

Jesus didn't need help sharing the gospel, but he asked for it anyway. First, he asked Simon, also called Peter, and Andrew. They were fishing when Jesus said to them "Come, follow me, and I will show you how to fish for people!" The Bible says they immediately left their nets and followed him!

Peter and Andrew were the first to become Jesus' disciples, but they weren't the last. That same day, just up the shore, they saw two brothers, James and John. James and John were also fishers, and they were in their boat with their father. When Jesus saw them, he asked James and John to follow him. Once again, they followed him immediately.

Jesus didn't just ask fishermen to help him. He asked all kinds of people, including a tax collector named Levi. Just like the other men, when Jesus asked Levi to be his disciple, Levi got up, left everything and followed Jesus.

Eventually, Jesus had twelve disciples who helped him share the gospel. What would you say if Jesus asked you to follow him?

discussion questions 💬

1. How many disciples did Jesus have?
2. What did each of the disciples do when Jesus asked them to follow him?

Let's Go Fishing

what you need 🖌

- String
- Stick, dowel, or ruler
- Magnets
- Scissors
- Crayons or markers
- Tape
- Paper clips

what you do ✂

Before class, photocopy this page, making one for each child. Make two fishing poles by tying a long string to a stick, dowel, or ruler. Tie a magnet on the other end of the string. After children decorate their fish, divide the group into two teams. Place a pile of fish in front of each team. Children hold fishing pole over the fish in an attempt to make the magnet and paper clip connect. After catching a fish, the player hands the pole to the next player. Continue until all fish are caught. The first team to catch all of its fish answers a discussion question.

what children do ✋

1. Cut out and decorate their fish.
2. Write your name on the back of your fish.
3. Tape a paper clip on the nose of the fish.

what to say 📣

Jesus often used familiar words and stories to teach people about God. When Jesus said the disciples would be fishing for people, they understood what he meant. Jesus wanted to teach them how to help people know God.

hole

finished craft

Jesus' Followers Scramble

what you need 🖌
- Crayons or markers

what you do ✂
Before class, photocopy this page, making one for each child.

what children do ✋
1. Unscramble the words below to learn the names of Jesus' 12 disciples.

what to say 📢
Jesus called twelve disciples to help him spread the Good News of the Gospel. These men had worked at many different jobs. They had to learn how to live a new kind of life. Jesus taught them through his words and his example. Jesus showed his disciples how to follow him.

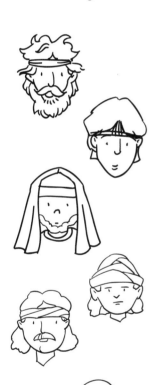

1. NMOSI TREPE _____

2. WADNER _____

3. SJMAE _____

4. NJHO _____

5. IPPHLI _____

6. LWROMTBEAHO _____

7. TWTMEAH _____

8. SMATOH _____

9. MEJAS _____

10. MIOSN _____

11. UDSAJ _____

12. ADUSJ CRSAITIO _____

Puffy Puff Paint Fish

what you need ✎

- Crayons or markers
- Scissors
- Paper or poster board
- Stapler
- Tissue paper
- Puff paints
- Paintbrushes
- Wiggle eyes or buttons

what you do ✂

Before class, photocopy this page, making one for each child.

what children do ✋

1. Trace and cut out two fish from paper or poster board.
2. Staple the two fish together, leaving the tails open.
3. Stuff tissue paper inside and staple the tails shut when the fish are puffy.
4. Decorate your fish using puff paints.
5. Glue wiggle eyes or buttons for eyes.

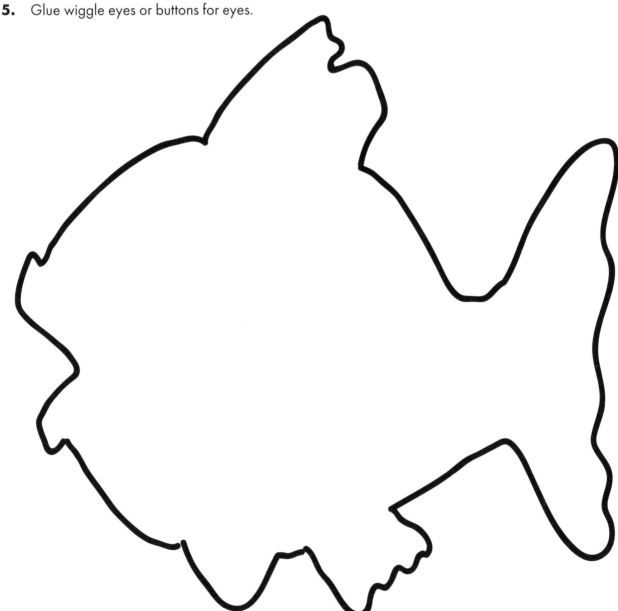

Jesus' Friends

Follow Me (based on Luke 5:1–11)

memory verse 📖

A real friend sticks closer than a brother.
Proverbs 18:24

discussion questions 💬

1. How many disciples did Jesus have?
2. What did each of the disciples do when Jesus asked them to follow him?

Follow Me Pasta Bracelet

Make a pasta bracelet with six pasta pieces and six bright-colored squares to remind you of the twelve disciples.

1. Cut out and color the sandals and squares. Use different colors for the squares.
2. Punch a hole on the sandals and on each square where indicated.
3. Cut a 14-inch length of yarn.
4. Thread the sandals to the center of the bracelet.
5. Add a piece of pasta to both sides of the sandals. Then add a colored square to both sides. Continue until you have three pieces of pasta and three squares on both sides of the sandals.
6. Ask someone to help you tie the bracelet onto your wrist.

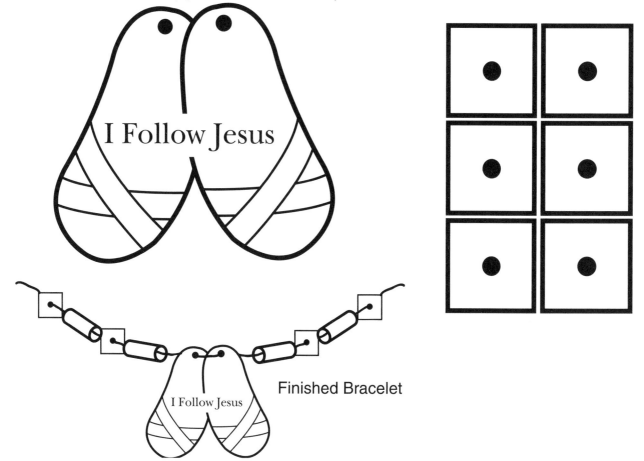

Finished Bracelet

Jesus Helps at a Wedding

memory verse 📖

Don't forget to do good.
Hebrews 13:16

The Wedding at Cana (based on John 2:1–11)

Jesus was a human, just like us. He worked, went to church, and attended celebrations, just like we do. One day, Jesus and his disciples were at a wedding in a town called Cana. His mother, Mary, was also there, helping with the celebration.

At one point, the wedding party ran out of wine. Mary asked Jesus to help. So Jesus asked some servants to fill six stone jars with water. Once the jars were full, Jesus told them to take some to the man in charge of the party. When he tasted it, it was wine! Jesus turned the water into wine.

This was the first miracle Jesus performed, but many more were to come. All of his miracles showed God's power and glory, helping those around him understand who he was.

discussion questions 💬

1. What was Jesus' first miracle?
2. How was Jesus able to turn the water into wine?

Who to Ask

what you need 🖊

- Crayons or markers

what you do ✂

Before class, photocopy this page, making one for each child.

what children do ✋

1. Use the code to reveal Mary's wise words. Write the letters in the blanks.
2. Unscramble the circled letters to learn how to find joy like the wedding guests felt after the miracle.

what to say 📢

When the refreshments ran out at the wedding at Cana, Mary knew what to do. She knew that Jesus could help. Mary's words tell us where to find the answers to our problems, too.

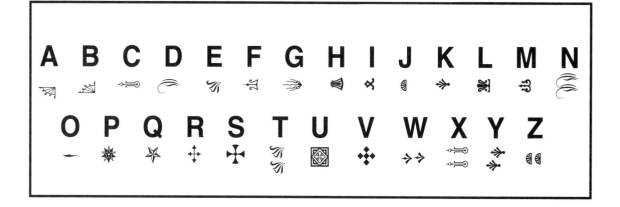

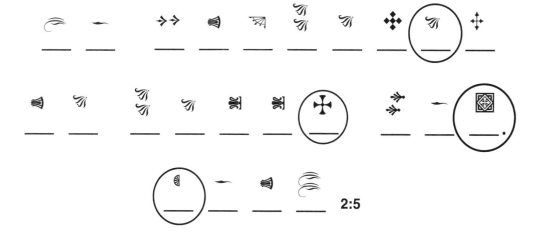

2:5

67

Color by Number Wedding

what you need ✎

- Crayons or markers

what you do ✂

Before class, photocopy this page, making one for each child.

what children do ✋

1. Follow the numbers to color the picture.

what to say 📢

We can always take our problems to Jesus. He will help us, just as he helped the wedding guests.

1= white
2= glue
3= brown
4= red
5= pink
6= green

What's Wrong Here

what you need ✎

- Crayons or markers

what you do ✂

Before class, photocopy this page, making one for each child.

what children do ✋

1. Color the picture.
2. Something is wrong with each picture on this page. Find and circle each wrong item.

what to say 📢

Sometimes things go wrong in our lives, too. When that happens, we can do our best to correct the wrong, and we can ask God for his help. Talking to God may not always correct the wrong, but God will give us the strength to cope with the wrong and to help others cope with it, too.

JUST CARRIED

Incorrect Objects: candy cane on candle holder, cup and spoon in bouquet, square wedding rings, mouse on cake, Just Carried sign, bride's veil is a net with fish, groom has only one eyebrow, groom's tie doesn't match, bride is frowning, bride has only one eye with eyelashes.

Jesus Helps at a Wedding

The Wedding at Cana (based on John 2:1–11)

memory verse

Don't forget to do good.
Hebrews 13:16

discussion questions

1. What was Jesus' first miracle?
2. How was Jesus able to turn the water into wine?

A Family of Do-Gooders

When Jesus helped at the wedding in Cana, he set an example for us to follow. As our memory verse reminds us, we should always remember to do good.

As a family, set a goal of "do-good" activities to complete this week. Set a realistic goal for the number of activities you will accomplish during the next seven days. Also, vote on a family prize if the goal is met: a special meal for dinner, family movie night, a new jigsaw puzzle to complete, a game of Frisbee at a local park, a trip to the beach—something special to enjoy together!

During the week, every evening at dinner, each family member shares ways that they were able to do good for someone else. Keep score. At the end of the week, if your family has met the goal, enjoy your prize!

Here are some ideas to get your family started on doing good things:

- Encourage someone or tell them "good job" after they've done a hard task.
- Send an encouraging card or text to someone who you know is sad or sick.
- Bake cookies and take them to the neighbors.
- Pray as a family for leaders, teachers, friends, family members, or others.
- Let someone go ahead of you in line.
- Get someone a drink of water without being asked.
- Put a bag of food in the car to give away to a homeless person when you see them.
- Leave a note of encouragement in a library book.
- Give a friend or family member a hug for no reason.
- Let someone else have the first turn playing a video game.
- Share a treasured item with someone else.

Woman at the Well

memory verse 📖

I will be glad and rejoice in your unfailing love.
Psalm 31:7

Jesus Knows Me & Loves Me (based on John 4:4–42)

Jesus was walking through Samaria on his way to Galilee. It was a long walk, so he stopped at a well around noontime. When a woman came to draw water from the well, he said to her, "Please give me a drink."

The Samaritan woman was surprised. "You are a Jew, and I am a Samaritan woman. Why are you asking me for a drink," she asked. Jewish people normally did not speak to Samaritans, and it wasn't normal during this time for men and women to speak together.

Then, Jesus said something that was strange to her. "If you knew who you were speaking to, you would ask me, and I would give you living water," he said. "Those who drink the water I give will never be thirsty again."

Living water? What's that, she wondered. She was interested, but Jesus had more to say. In fact, it turned out that Jesus knew all about her. He told her things about her life that only she knew. Who was this man, she wondered. "You must be a prophet," she said.

Jesus told her, "I AM the Messiah!"

Finally, the woman understood—she was speaking to the Savior! The woman was amazed! She began worshiping Jesus there at the well, and when she returned home, she told everyone she met that she had spoken to Jesus, the Savior God promised.

discussion questions 💬

1. What was the living water Jesus offered?
2. How can we have living water today?

Dot-to-Dot Surprise

what you need 🖌

- Crayons or markers

what you do ✂

Before class, photocopy this page, making one for each child.

what to say 📢

Where would the woman hold the living water Jesus would give her? Complete the dot-to-dot to find out!

what children do ✋

1. Follow the dots to find the answer.
2. Draw blue water around what you found and color it with your favorite color.

Well Pencil Holder

what you need ✏

- Crayons or markers
- Scissors
- Glue
- Clean, empty cans, one per child
- Blue paint
- Paintbrushes
- Yarn
- Ruler

what you do ✂

Before class, photocopy this page, making one for each child. Wash out empty cans, one per child. Cut yarn into five-inch lengths.

what children do ✋

1. Color and cut out the water jug.
2. Paint the inside of the water jug with blue paint and allow to dry.
3. Color and cut out the stone well.
4. Glue the well around a can.
5. Glue the yarn around the top of the juice can and between the front and back of the water jug.

Jesus Gives Living Water
(John 4:1-42)

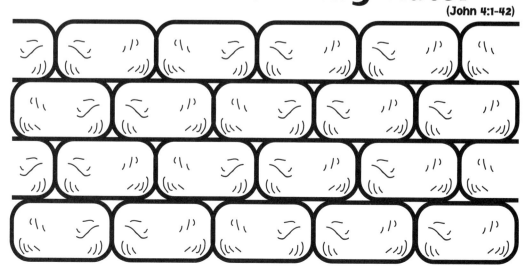

W Is for Water

what you need ✏
- Pencils

what you do ✂
Before class, photocopy this page, making one for each child.

what children do ✋
Fill in the blanks with the letter W to complete the story.

Narrator: Jesus _____anted _____ater from a _____ell.
He asked a _____oman for __ater from the _____ell.

_____oman: _____hy are you asking me for _____ater?"

Jesus: If you knew _____ho I _____as you _____ould ask me
for _____ater. I _____ill give you living _____ater."

Narrator: The _____oman _____hined . . .

_____oman: I _____ant living _____ater. But _____hy do your people say to
_____orship God in Jerusalem? _____e _____orship God on a mountain.

Jesus: God _____ants you to _____orship in spirit and in truth.

_____oman: _____hen the Savior of the _____orld comes,
he _____ill help us understand everything.

Jesus: I am the person _____ho you speak of.

Narrator: The _____oman left her _____ater jar at the _____
ell and ran back to town. She told everyone:

_____oman: Come meet a man _____ho told me
everything I ever did. Could this be the Savior?

Narrator: _____hen the people met Jesus, they
said to the _____oman at the _____ell:

Townspeople: _____e no longer believe just because of _____hat
you said; now _____e have heard for ourselves and _____e
know that this man really is the Savior of the _____orld."

 Top 50 Bible Stories about Jesus for Elementary.

Woman at the Well

Jesus Knows Me & Loves Me (based on John 2:1–11)

memory verse 📖

I will be glad and rejoice in your unfailing love.
Psalm 31:7

discussion questions 💬

1. What was the living water Jesus offered?
2. How can we have living water today?

The Hidden Message

What would Jesus' water satisfy? Find the answer in the picture below. If the first condition is true, color the spaces indicated. If not, then go to the next bullet.

- If the sun is yellow, color spaces *A* and *E* red.
- If apples are purple, color spaces *B* and *F* green.
- If grapes are green, color spaces *C* and *G* blue.
- If milk is pink, color spaces *D* and *H* blue.
- If oranges are orange color spaces *B* and *I* brown.

- If water is wet, color *L*, *D*, and *F* red.
- If cows give chocolate milk, color spaces *I* and *K* orange.
- If grass is magenta, color the remaining spaces green. If not, color them yellow.

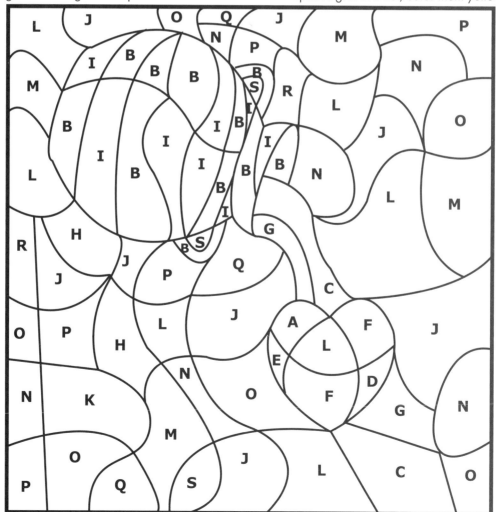

Four Friends Carry a Friend to See Jesus

memory verse 📖

We should do good to everyone.
Galatians 6:10

Down through the Roof (based on Mark 2:1–12)

Jesus performed many miracles. News of his works made people more and more curious about who he was. Everywhere he went, crowds of people seemed to form around him, hoping to see and hear more.

Sometimes, the crowds around Jesus made it difficult for people to get to him. One time, at a house in Capernaum, so many people came to listen that there was no room inside or around the house. While Jesus was preaching, four men came carrying a paralyzed man on a mat. They wanted him to meet Jesus so he could be healed.

How do you think these men got their friend to Jesus through the crowd? They cut a hole into the roof and lowered the man down on his mat, right where Jesus was preaching!

Jesus saw how faithful the men were to bring their friend for healing, so he told the paralyzed man, "My child, your sins are forgiven."

Some people didn't like this, though. They said only God could forgive sins. They didn't realize that Jesus IS God. To show them his power, Jesus turned to the paralyzed man and said, "Stand up, pick up your mat, and go home!"

Suddenly, the man was healed! He got up, grabbed his mat, and walked around. The people were amazed. Surely this man is the Son of God, they thought.

discussion questions 💬

1. Why did the four men bring their friend to Jesus?
2. Why were some people upset that Jesus told the man his sins were forgiven?

Secret Code of Praise

what you need ✎

- Crayons or markers

what you do ✂

Before class, photocopy this page, making one for each child.

what children do ✋

1. Using the code below, find out what the five men did on their way home.
2. When you're done, sing the song below about being a good friend.

what to say 📢

When Jesus saw how hard the man's friends had worked, he told the sick man to get up. "Stand up, take your mat and walk home," he said. The man obeyed Jesus. Everyone who witnessed the healing was amazed. They said, "We've never seen anything like this before!"

A=$ D=&   E=+   G=J   I=@   O=<   P=?   R=*   S=>

The five men ___ ___ ___ ___ ___ ___ ___   ___ ___ ___

             ?   * $ @   >   +   &   J   <   &

Now sing this song to the tune of "B-I-N-G-O."

A sick man had four good friends,

They took him to see Je-sus!

F-R-I-E-N-D, F-R-I-E-N-D, F-R-I-E-N-D,

They took him to see Je-sus!

Jesus healed that poor, sick man,

They walked home saying, "Thank You!"

P-R-A-I-S-E, P-R-A-I-S-E, P-R-A-I-S-E,

They walked home saying, "Thank You!"

I Can Help Reminder

what you need ✐

- Scissors
- Crayons or markers
- Paper
- Glue

what you do ✂

Before class, photocopy this page, making one for each child.

what to say 📢

The paralyzed man had special friends, didn't he? They could have said there wasn't any way they could get him to Jesus. They could have turned back because the house was full. After Jesus healed the man, his friends must have been glad they persisted in getting him to Jesus. Make this craft to remind yourself that you can help others.

what children do ✋

1. Write "I can help" on the strip pattern and color the face to look like you.
2. Cut out the patterns.
3. Trace both of your hands on a piece of paper.
4. Color and cut out both hands.
5. Glue your right hand to the right side of the strip pattern and your left hand to the left side.
6. Glue the bottom of the face to the top-center of the strip.

Four Friends Scrambler

what you need ✏

- Pencils

what you do ✂

Before class, photocopy this page, making one for each child.

what children do ✋

You can find the story of the four men who brought their friend to Jesus in Mark 2:1–12.
To retell the story, unscramble the scrambled words on the blank lines.

1. Jesus was visiting Cmuarenpa _____.

2. Four men brought their ndfire _____, who could not walk, to Jesus.

3. Because of the dcorw _____, the four men could not reach Jesus.

4. They carried their friend up to the oorf _____ of the shuoe _____.

5. The friends made a hole in the roof and owlreed _____

   their friend to the feet of Jesus.

6. Jesus eahdel _____ the man and

   gfrovae _____ his sins.

7. The people were maazde _____.

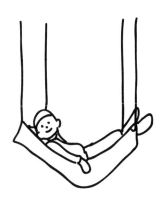

Four Friends Carry a Friend to See Jesus

Down through the Roof (based on Mark 2:1–12)

memory verse 📖

We should do good to everyone.
Galatians 6:10

discussion questions 💬

1. Why did the four men bring their friend to Jesus?
2. Why were some people upset that Jesus told the man his sins were forgiven?

"Friend of the Year" Game

The friends of the paralyzed man were determined to take him to Jesus. They should have been given the "Friend of the Year" award. Play the game with a friend or two and see who becomes "Friend of the Year." You will need buttons for markers and number cubes to find out how many squares to move.

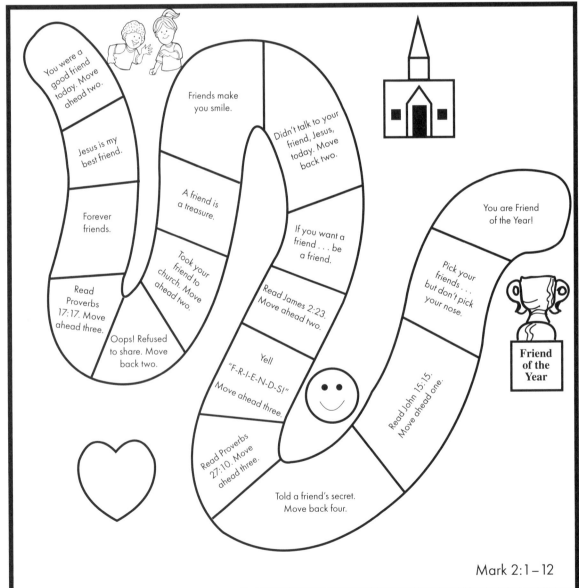

You were a good friend today. Move ahead two.

Jesus is my best friend.

Forever friends.

Read Proverbs 17:17. Move ahead three.

Oops! Refused to share. Move back two.

Friends make you smile.

A friend is a treasure.

Took your friend to church. Move ahead two.

Read Proverbs 27:10. Move ahead three.

Yell "F-R-I-E-N-D-S!" Move ahead three.

Didn't talk to your friend, Jesus, today. Move back two.

If you want a friend . . . be a friend.

Read James 2:23. Move ahead two.

Told a friend's secret. Move back four.

Read John 15:15. Move ahead one.

You are Friend of the Year!

Pick your friends . . . but don't pick your nose.

Friend of the Year

Mark 2:1–12

Jesus Teaches Us to Be Happy

memory verse 📖

God gives wisdom, knowledge, and joy to those who please him.
Ecclesiastes 2:26

The Sermon on the Mount (based on Matthew 5:3–12)

When Jesus was a man, he began preaching and teaching to large crowds who came to hear him. Jesus' disciples wrote down his sermons. These sermons and teachings are in the first four books of the Bible we call the Gospels, which means good news.

One sermon Jesus gave is called the Sermon on the Mount. It's found in the Book of Matthew. The Sermon on the Mount is one of Jesus' most famous sermons because of all the good things it has to say. During this sermon, Jesus taught us how to live a happy Christian life.

"Happy are those who know they need God. Happy are those who receive God's comfort. Happy are those who help others, try to be fair, show kindness, and make peace. Happy are those who show they belong to God's family, even if others are mean to them.

"Be happy! Be glad! You will receive a great prize in Heaven some day."

It might be surprising to hear what Jesus said in the Sermon on the Mount. How can we be happy when others are mean to us?

Jesus teaches us that we can rely completely on him. It might be difficult at times, but we can trust him to lead our lives right.

discussion

questions 💬

1. What is one way Jesus said we can be happy from the Sermon on the Mount?
2. How can we be happy, even if others are mean to us?

Find the Right Smile

what you need 🖌
- Crayons or markers

what you do ✂
Before class, photocopy this page, making one for each child.

what children do ✋
1. Look at the first phrase. Find the matching second part in the set below it.
2. Color each pair of smiling faces with a different color.
3. Continue until all phrases are matched. For answers, read Matthew 5:3–12.

what to say 📢
Jesus wants us to be happy in spite of the not-so-good things that happen in our lives. You might not always feel like smiling, but you can still have a joyful heart because you know Jesus will help you when you have problems.

1. God blesses those who are poor and realize their need for him.

2. God blesses those who mourn.

3. God blesses those who are humble.

4. God blesses those who hunger and thirst for justice.

5. God blesses those who are merciful.

6. God blesses those whose hearts are pure.

7. God blesses those who work for peace.

8. God blesses those who are persecuted for doing right.

A. For they will be satisfied.

B. For the Kingdom of Heaven is theirs.

C. For they will be comforted.

D. For they will be called the children of God.

E. For the Kingdom of Heaven is theirs.

F. For they will see God.

G. For they will inherit the whole earth.

H. For they will be shown mercy.

Happy Game

what you need ✏

- Crayons or markers
- Scissors
- Paper bags, one per group

what you do ✂

Before class, photocopy this page, making one for each child. During class, divide children into groups of three or four. Choose one person from each group to go first.

what children do ✋

1. Color the face your favorite color.
2. Cut out the face and face pieces.

how to play ✋

1. Players keep their face boards but put all face pieces into their group's bag.
2. Starting with the first player, draw a face piece from the bag and choose whether to put it on your board. The goal is to be the first to collect all four pieces.
3. If you don't already have that face piece, you can take it. Place the piece on your board and continue to the next person. If you already have the piece you drew, put the piece back in the bag and continue to the next person.
4. If you draw a frown (down arrow), skip your turn.
5. The first to collect all four pieces answers a discussion question.

Matthew 5:3–12

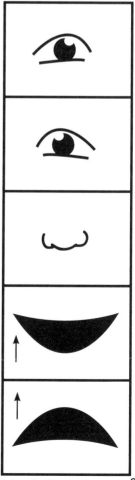

Be-Attitudes Poster

what you need ✏

- Crayons or markers
- Scissors
- Construction paper
- Glue
- Wiggle eyes
- Elbow macaroni

what you do ✂

Before class, photocopy this page, making one for each child.

what children do ✋

1. Color the faces.
2. Cut out the faces below.
3. Glue the face papers to a sheet of construction paper to make a poster.
4. Glue wiggle eyes to the eyes and macaroni on the mouth.
5. Display the poster in your room to remind you of Jesus' sermon.

Jesus Teaches Us to Be Happy

The Sermon on the Mount (based on Matthew 5:3–12)

memory verse 📖

God gives wisdom, knowledge, and joy to those who please him.
Ecclesiastes 2:26

discussion questions 💬

1. What is one way Jesus said we can be happy from the Sermon on the Mount?
2. How can we be happy, even if others are mean to us?

Eat the Word

Read Jeremiah 15:16. Jeremiah was saying that just as a full stomach makes him happy, so does a full heart when he reads about God and his law. This bookmark will help you remember to "eat" the Bible this week. Feed your spiritual hunger with Bible verses.

Color the bookmark and cut it out. As you read the verses each day, put a check in the box by the Scripture text. Write your favorite verse from the week in the space at the bottom of the bookmark.

❏ Sunday – Psalm 1:2

❏ Monday – Psalm 119:165

❏ Tuesday – Joshua 1:8

❏ Wednesday – Psalm 119:9

❏ Thursday – Psalm 40:8

❏ Friday – Psalm 19:7

❏ Saturday – Psalm 119:11

Jesus Teaches Us about Salt & Light

memory verse 📖

Let your good deeds shine out for all to see, so that everyone will praise your heavenly Father.
Matthew 5:16

The Light of the World (based on Matthew 5:13–16; Luke 14:34–35)

What would you say if someone told you, "You are the salt of the earth"? Would you know what they meant? What if they also said, "You are the light of the world"? Would that give you a better idea?

This is what Jesus told his followers one day. He told them to be salt and to be a light. Some of them might have been confused by what Jesus said. But he had a reason for the way he spoke.

Jesus spoke in ways that the people of his time would understand. In Bible times, salt was very important. Salt helps preserve meat, keeping it fresh and preventing it from rotting. It also gives things great flavor. Jesus asked, "What good is salt if it has lost its flavor?" Salt without flavor is useless! So Jesus wants us to be salt that is pure and full of flavor. We're like salt when we listen to God and obey him, when we pray and do good works for others.

Jesus also said that we should be a light. Not just any light, though. Jesus said we should be a light that cannot be hidden. This means that our love for Jesus should show for everyone to see! People will be able to see that we love God by how we live.

Being salt and light isn't something we can do on our own. We can only follow God by loving Jesus. We can pray to Jesus for help, and he will help us show God's love to everyone we see.

discussion questions 💬

1. What did Jesus mean when he said "You are the salt of the earth"?
2. How can we be a light?

Pick a Picture Story

what you need ✒

- Crayons or markers

what you do ✂

Before class, photocopy this page, making one for each child.

what children do ✋

1. Read through the story below.
2. Choose the picture that fits in each sentence. Draw that picture in the space. You may use the picture more than once.

what to say 📢

The story of the lighted candle contains many beautiful pictures of how God wants us to live. With God's love inside of us, we are like lights that can chase away the darkness of loneliness and fear. We shine with the Good News of the Gospel of Jesus Christ.

You are the _____ of the _____—

like a _____ on a _____ that

cannot be hidden. No one lights a _____

and then puts it under a _____. Instead, a

_____ is placed on a stand, where it gives

_____ to everyone in the _____. In the

same way, let your good deeds shine out for _____ to see,

so that everyone will praise your _____ly Father.

Matthew 5:14–16

Go Salt the World

what you need 🖌

- Table covering
- Plastic cups
- Salt
- Food coloring, several colors
- Scissors
- Glue
- Hole punch
- Fishing line

what you do ✂

Before class, photocopy this page, making one for each child. Cover tables with table covering. Make the colored salt by pouring salt into plastic cups, one cup per color. Mix a few drops of food coloring into each cup. Adjust amounts to make colors lighter or darker.

what children do ✋

1. Cut out the verse plaque.
2. Spread a thin layer of glue on one of the letters.
3. Sprinkle with the colored salt. Tap the picture lightly to remove unglued salt.
4. Repeat for each letter and the Earth picture.
5. Punch holes in the top where indicated.
6. Thread and tie fishing line in the holes so you can hang your motto.

what to say 📢

Jesus tells us that we should salt the world. If your friend sees you responding with a bad attitude, an unkind spirit or grumpiness, your salt has lost its flavor. Look up one of these Scriptures as a quick reminder! Make this salt motto as another way to remind you to be salty.

GO SALT the 🌍

(Luke 14:34-35)

A Salty Snack

what you need 🖌

- Large bowl
- 5 cups of popped popcorn
- Cup of pretzel sticks, broken in half
- Cup of peanuts
- Cup of raisins
- ½ cup measure
- Paper plates or bowls

what you do ✂

Before class, mix everything together in a large bowl. Use a ½ cup measure to pour onto paper plates or bowls. The recipe will make sixteen servings. Ask children the discussion questions as they snack.

what to say 📢

Jesus told us that we are to be the salt of the world. Salt seasons our food and makes it taste better. But when the salt doesn't taste salty, it isn't good for anything; we might as well throw it out!

Jesus used objects to teach his disciples and friends how to live a Christian life. This salty snack reminds us to keep our Christian life fresh so we will make our friends hungry for Jesus.

discussion questions 💬

1. What did Jesus mean when he said "You are the salt of the earth"?
2. What are some ways you can be salt at home? At school? When you're with your friends?
3. How can we be a light?
4. What is one thing you can do today to be a light for others?

Jesus Teaches Us about Salt & Light

The Light of the World (based on Matthew 5:13–16; Luke 14:34–35)

memory verse 📖

Let your good deeds shine out for all to see, so that everyone will praise your heavenly Father.
Matthew 5:16

discussion questions 💬

1. What did Jesus mean when he said "You are the salt of the earth"?
2. How can we be a light?

Paper Lantern

Make a paper lantern to remind you of Jesus' words. Cut and fold the lantern as shown.

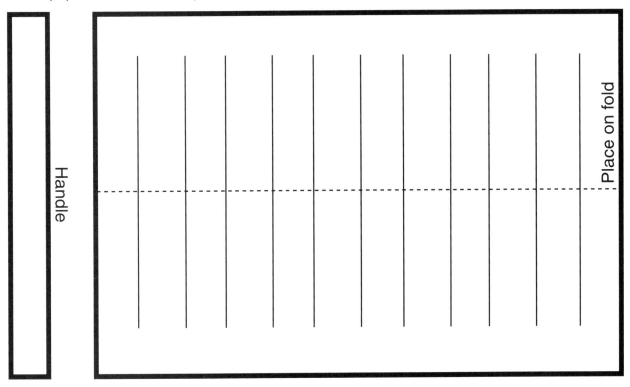

Handle

Place on fold

1.

2. Open & fold lengthwise.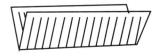

3. Open.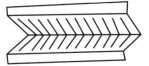

4. Glue or tape edges.

5. Glue on handle and trim.

6. Tape yellow tissue paper inside for light.

Jesus Teaches Us about Birds & Flowers

memory verse

Seek the Kingdom of God above all else, and live righteously, and he will give you everything you need.
Matthew 6:33

Happy Birds, Beautiful Flowers (based on Matthew 6:25–34)

What are some things you worry about? Do you worry about food or what you eat? Do you worry about what you wear?

Sometimes we worry too much about these things. Other times we make these things too important. We worry about having the best clothes or the tastiest food.

Food and clothing are things we need, but Jesus doesn't want us to worry about them.

"Look at the birds," Jesus said. "They don't plant or harvest or store food in barns, for your heavenly Father feeds them. And aren't you far more valuable to him than they are?"

Jesus also said, "Look at the lilies of the field and how they grow. They don't work or make their clothing, yet Solomon in all his glory was not dressed as beautifully as they are."

Since we have God in our lives, we don't have to worry about these things. We can be like the birds and the flowers because God has already given us everything we need through Jesus.

All we have to do is seek Jesus. If Jesus is our friend, he will take care of what we need.

discussion questions

1. What are some ways God takes care of his creation?
2. What are some ways God takes care of you?

Flower Bookmark

what you need

- Scissors
- Crayons or markers
- Glue
- Hole punch
- Yarn

what you do ✂

Before class, photocopy this page, making one for each child.

what children do ✋

1. Color and cut out the bookmark pattern.
2. Color and cut out flowers to glue on the bookmarks. Choose the flowers you will make and the colors you will use. Arrange them in your own design.
3. Punch a hole in the top and tie a piece of yarn through it.

Look at the lilies of the field and how they grow.

Matthew 6:28

Flying Bird

what you need ✎

- Craft knife (adult use only)
- Crayons or markers
- Scissors
- Paper
- Glue
- Hole punch
- Ribbon

what you do ✂

Before class, photocopy this page, making one for each child. Use a craft knife to cut a slit on the line on each bird. Cut strips of ribbon, various lengths.

what children do ✋

1. Color and cut out bird, eyes, and wing template.
2. Fold a piece of paper in half.
3. Place the wing template on the folded sheet of paper as indicated and trace.
4. Cut out the wings and insert them through the slit in the bird.
5. Glue on the eyes and decorate as you wish.
6. Glue strips of ribbon to the tail.
7. Punch a pole on the black dot and add a ribbon hanger.

God cares for me.
Matthew 6:25–34

Place on fold

Finished Bird

Flower Chain

what you need ✐

- Ribbon
- Ruler
- Scissors
- White, yellow, and green construction paper
- Glue
- Tape

what you do ✂

Before class, photocopy this page, making one for each child. Cut ribbon into 4½-foot lengths, one for each child.

what children do ✋

1. Cut out the flower, center, and leaf templates.
2. On construction paper, use the templates to trace and cut out two white flowers, ten yellow centers, and ten green leaves.
3. Glue a yellow center in each flower. Glue a leaf behind each flower.
4. Lay the ribbon on a table and tape the daisies along the ribbon about four inches apart from center to center. Leave five inches at each end for tying the chain.

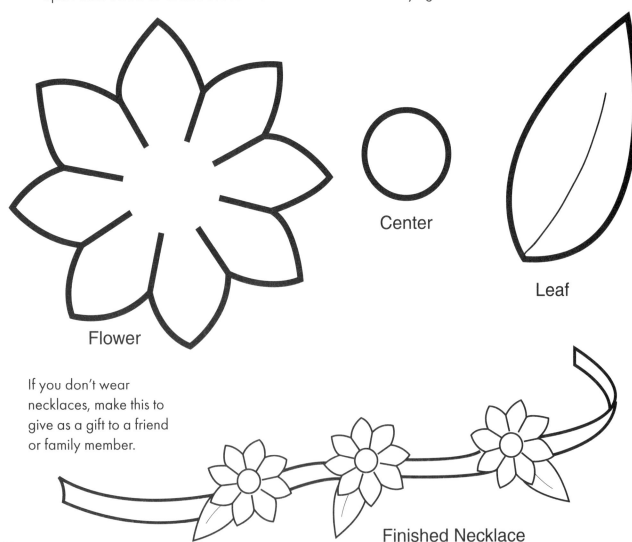

Flower

Center

Leaf

If you don't wear necklaces, make this to give as a gift to a friend or family member.

Finished Necklace

Jesus Teaches Us about Birds & Flowers

Happy Birds, Beautiful Flowers (based on Matthew 6:25–34)

memory verse 📖

Seek the Kingdom of God above all else, and live righteously, and he will give you everything you need.
Matthew 6:33

discussion questions 💬

1. What are some ways God takes care of his creation?
2. What are some ways God takes care of you?

Bird Code

What kind of bird did Jesus use in this Bible lesson? What did he say God knew about this bird? Solve the code below to find the answers. The first number represents the column; the second number is the number of spaces down. Write the letters on the lines. Example: 4/4 = W (4th column from left, 4th letter down).

1	2	3	4	5	6	7	8	9	10	11	12	13	14
P	O	B	C	B	D	G	H	F	M	R	Q	S	P
A	W	L	R	O	O	O	A	A	O	O	U	N	I
R	L	A	O	V	O	L	W	L	C	B	A	O	G
T		C	W	E		D	K	C	K	I	I	W	E
R		K	H			F		O	I	N	L	B	O
I		B	I			I		N	N			I	N
D		I	T			N			G			R	
G		R	E			C			B			D	
E		D				H			I				
									R				
									D				

___ ___ ___ ___ ___ ___ ___ ___ ; ___ ___ ___
13/1 14/1 8/2 10/10 1/5 6/2 5/4   7/1 4/3 3/9

___ ___ ___ ___   ___ ___ ___ ___ Y ___ ___ ___
13/1 6/4 5/8 13/1   14/4 6/3 1/9 11/1   9/5 11/5 6/4

___ ___ ___ ___   ___ ___ ___ ___ ___
1/4 7/9 12/3 5/7   7/5 8/2 9/3 7/3 13/1

___ ___   ___ ___ ___   ___ ___ ___ ___ ___ ___ .
1/4 2/1   5/7 8/1 6/4   10/7 4/2 11/2 12/2 14/6 13/8

The House on a Rock

memory verse 📖

Don't just listen to God's word. You must do what it says.
James 1:22

Wise Men Obey God's Word (based on Matthew 7:24–27)

One day Jesus told his followers a story about two men. Each man was building a house, but they went about it differently.

The first man built his house on solid rock. Because the ground below him was firm, the house was strong and sturdy. The second man built his house on sand. Have you ever been to the beach or played in a sandbox? Sand is always moving! It's not strong like solid rock.

What do you think happened when it rained and flooded? The man who built his house on solid rock was fine. His house didn't collapse because it had a sturdy foundation. But the house built on sand collapsed to the ground. The sand wasn't strong enough to support it in the storm!

Jesus told his followers that anyone who listens to him is like the man who built his house on solid rock. Jesus' teachings help make us strong believers. With Jesus, even the strongest storm can't knock us down.

discussion questions 💬

1. What was the difference between the man who built on solid rock and the man who built on sand?
2. How can we be wise like the man who built his house on solid rock?

Choose a Word Quiz

what you need ✐

- Crayons or markers

what you do ✂

Before class, photocopy this page, making one for each child.

what children do ✋

1. Write the correct letter beside each statement. You will use answer D twice.
2. Fill in the blanks at the bottom of the page with the first eight letters to complete the sentence.

what to say 📢

Jesus used parables or stories to help people understand more about God. This story of two builders shows how important it is to love God's Word and follow its teachings. When sad things happen or hard times come, we can feel safe and secure in God's care.

_____ 1. Name the two kinds of men in this story.

_____ 2. Name the two kinds of foundations on which the men built their homes.

_____ 3. What does the Bible say first descended on both houses after they were built?

_____ 4. What happened to the house on the rock during the storm?

_____ 5. Which kind of person does the wise builder of the house on the rock represent?

_____ 6. What happened to the house on the sand during the storm?

_____ 7. Which kind of person does the foolish builder of the house on the sand represent?

_____ 8. Would you rather be a person who believes or refuses God's Word?

_____ 9. Is a person who listens to Jesus and obeys him wise or foolish?

_____ 10. Where did the wise man build his house?

_____ 11. Is a person who listens to Jesus and does not obey Him wise or foolish?

_____ 12. Where did the foolish man build his house?

_____ 13. What are the other two things that hit both houses after they were built?

_____ 14. Who is telling this parable story?

A. on the sand
B. winds and floods
C. wise and foolish
D. one who believes and follows God's Word
E. foolish
F. Jesus
G. it fell

H. rock and sand
I. rain
J. on a rock
K. wise
L. it remained standing
O. One who hears God's Word, but refuses it

I am a __ __ __ __ of __ __ __.

Who Lives in this House?

what you need ✎

- Crayons or markers

what you do ✂

Before class, photocopy this page, making one for each child.

what children do ✋

1. Look at the pictures below.
2. Draw a line from the owner to the correct house.
3. Color the pictures.

what to say 📢

Animals cannot choose what kinds of houses they will live in like people can. Some live in houses that God has planned for them to build, such as how birds build nests. Others live in houses that people build for them, such as barns for cows and pens for pigs

Picture Puzzle

what you need ✏

- Scissors
- Glue

what you do ✂

Before class, photocopy this page, making one for each child.

what children do ✋

1. Cut apart the pictures at the bottom of the page.
2. Some words are missing from the story below. Glue the pictures in the blank places to complete the story of the house on a rock.
3. Tell the story to a friend or a member of your family.

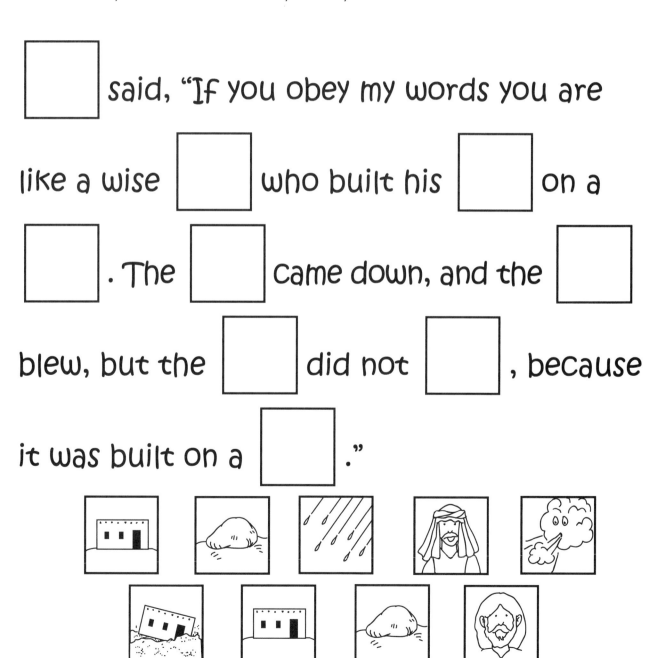

☐ said, "If you obey my words you are like a wise ☐ who built his ☐ on a ☐ . The ☐ came down, and the ☐ blew, but the ☐ did not ☐ , because it was built on a ☐ ."

The House on a Rock

Wise Men Obey God's Word (based on Matthew 7:24–27)

memory verse 📖

Don't just listen to God's word. You must do what it says.
James 1:22

discussion questions 💬

1. What was the difference between the man who built on solid rock and the man who built on sand?
2. How can we be wise like the man who built his house on solid rock?

The Sturdy House

Color the tools to remind you of the house built on a rock.

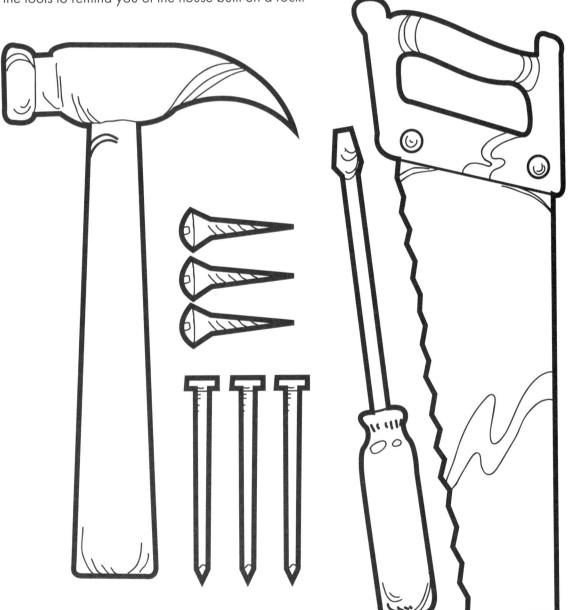

Jesus Calms the Sea

memory verse 📖

Praise the name of God forever and ever, for he has all wisdom and power.
Daniel 2:20

Jesus Is Powerful (based on Mark 4:35–41; Luke 8:22–25)

One day, Jesus and his disciples needed to cross a big lake. Crowds of people had been following them all day, and Jesus was tired. So they found a boat and set sail.

Once they were on the water, Jesus went to the back of the boat and fell asleep.

Soon, a big storm filled the sky. Giant waves crashed against the sides of the boat. It was starting to fill with water!

The disciples were scared. They shouted at Jesus to wake him up. "Don't you know that we're going to drown?"

Jesus woke up, saw the wind and the waves, and said "Silence! Be still!"

At once, the wind and the waves stopped. Everything was calm. Then Jesus asked his disciples, "Why are you afraid? Do you still have no faith?"

The disciples were still scared. They couldn't understand how Jesus stopped the storm. "Who is this man," they asked. "Even the winds and waves obey him!"

discussion questions 💬

1. How was Jesus able to calm the storm?
2. Why do you think the disciples were surprised that Jesus could calm a storm?

Jesus Calms the Sea

what you need

- Crayons or markers

what you do ✂

Before class, photocopy this page, making one for each child.

what children do ✋

1. Use the Morse Code Key below to decipher the Morse code. Each letter is separated by a slash.
2. Write each letter in order on the lines below the codes.

what to say 🔊

People used to use Morse Code to send messages when they had problems at sea. When you have a problem, you can pray to Jesus to help.

1 - -./- - -

_____

2 _. . ./- - -/.-/-

_____

3 . -/. . ./- - ./././- - -

_____

4 . . ./-/- - -/. - ./- -

_____

5 . . - ./././ - ./. - .

_____

6 . - -/ - - -/- . -/.

_____

7 .../. - ./ - - -/- . -/.

_____

8 - . -./. - ./- . ./- -

_____

9 . -/- - ./. - ./- - . ./././- . .

_____

10 - - - / - . . ./././- . - -

_____

MORSE CODE KEY

A . -	H	O - - -	V . . . -
B - . . .	I . .	P . - - .	W . - -
C - . - .	J . - - -	Q - - . -	X - . . -
D - . .	K - . -	R . - .	Y - . - -
E .	L . - . .	S . . .	Z - - . .
F . . - .	M - -	T -	
G - - .	N - .	U . . -	

Drama at Sea Quiz

what you need 🖌

- Red and blue crayons or markers
- Drinking straws, two for each child
- Scissors
- Tape

what you do ✂

Before class, photocopy this page, making one for each child. Read each question below. Give time between each question for children to raise their flags. Review each correct answer as you go.

what children do ✋

1. Color the center diamond of the *F* flag red. Color the left section of the *T* flag red and the right section blue. Leave the middle section white.
2. Cut out the flags.
3. Tape each flag to a straw.
4. Follow along as you hear the sentences below. If the statement is false, raise the *F* flag. If the statement is true, raise the *T* flag.

what to say 📢

Ships at sea use different flags to send messages. Today, you'll make the international flags for *T* and *F* for the Drama at Sea quiz.

1. Jesus and his disciples always stayed in one place.
2. The disciples went with Jesus on a bus.
3. Boats provided a faster, easier way to travel.
4. Jesus stayed awake on the boat to tell everyone what to do.
5. The weather grew stormy, and the sea got rough.
6. Water splashed in the boat until it was about to sink.
7. The disciples always trusted God and never felt afraid.
8. They yelled for Jesus to wake up and help them.
9. Jesus said, "Go away and let me sleep."
10. Jesus said, "Let's jump out of the boat and swim for shore."
11. Jesus came to their rescue quickly.
12. Jesus calmed the stormy wind and water.
13. Jesus told the disciples he was glad they panicked.
14. Jesus asked, "Where are your fishing nets?"
15. Jesus asked, "Where is your faith?"
16. The disciples thought nothing of the miracle.
17. The disciples felt great amazement at Jesus' power.
18. They all asked, "What shall we have for lunch?"
19. The disciples asked each other who Jesus really was.
20. They called a press conference when they reached shore.

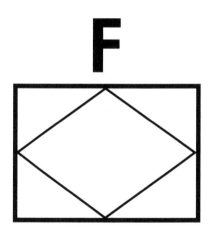

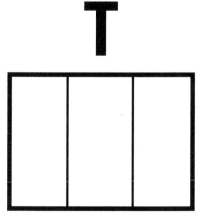

How Did Jesus Travel?

what you need 🖌

- Crayons or markers

what you do ✂

Before class, photocopy this page, making one for each child.

what children do ✋

1. Color each picture showing a way to travel.
2. If Jesus and his disciples could not have traveled that way, draw an *X* over the picture.
3. If they could have traveled that way, draw a line from Jesus to the way he traveled.
4. Circle the types of travel you have used.

what to say 📢

Jesus and his disciples often traveled by boat. Sometimes they walked from town to town. They wanted to tell the Good News everywhere, to everyone they met.

Jesus Calms the Sea

Jesus Is Powerful (based on Matthew 7:24–27)

memory verse 📖

Praise the name of God forever and ever, for he has all wisdom and power.
Daniel 2:20

discussion questions 💬

1. How was Jesus able to calm the storm?
2. Why do you think the disciples were surprised that Jesus could calm a storm?

Jesus' Boat

1. Cut a 6-inch paper plate cut in half.
2. Color and cut out the sail.
3. Glue the sail to a craft stick.
4. Glue the craft stick to the inside of one of the plate halves.
5. Cut out the people holder strip and the Scripture box.
6. Use tape to attach the people holder strip to the inside of the other plate half (see diagram).
7. Leaving the flat side of each plate open, glue the plate halves together with the people holder strip inside.
8. Draw faces onto two plastic spoons and place them into the people holder strips

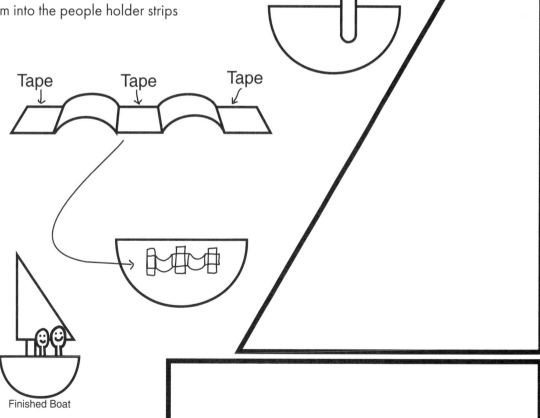

Tape   Tape   Tape

Sail

Finished Boat

People Holder Pattern

Jesus Heals Jairus's Daughter

memory verse

Anything is possible if a person believes.
Mark 9:23

Loving Kindness (based on Mark 5:21–43, Luke 8:40–56)

Crowds followed Jesus nearly everywhere he went. People wanted to know more about this man who did amazing things. Others wanted to be near him for healing or teaching.

A man named Jairus came to Jesus in the crowds one day. He fell at Jesus' feet and asked him to visit his house so he could heal his daughter.

Jesus agreed to help Jairus. But on his way, he stopped to heal another woman. While Jesus was healing her, a messenger came from Jairus's house. The messenger told Jairus that his daughter had died, so there was no need for Jesus to come.

But Jesus told Jairus, "Don't be afraid. Just have faith, and she will be healed."

Many people were gathered to mourn at Jairus's house when Jesus arrived. "Stop the weeping!" Jesus told them. "She's only asleep." The people were confused. They didn't believe him.

Then, Jesus went into the room where the girl was lying. In a loud voice, Jesus said, "My child, get up!"

Instantly, the girl awoke! She stood up, and her parents got her something to eat. Everyone was amazed! Jesus healed the girl, just as he had promised.

discussion questions

1. What did Jairus ask Jesus to do?
2. What did Jesus say Jairus needed to have for his daughter to be healed?

Jesus Heals Maze

what you need ✎

- Pencils

what you do ✂

Before class, photocopy this page, making one for each child.

what children do 🖐

Draw a path from Jesus in the upper right corner, past the people who doubted Jesus, to Jairus' daughter, whom Jesus brought back to life.

START

FINISH

A Father Asks for Help

what you need ✎
- Crayons or markers

what you do ✂
Before class, photocopy this page, making one for each child.

what children do ✋
Use the color code to color the spaces and find an important message.

- ■ Blue
- ● Red

A Father's Faith

what you need ✏

- Pencils

what you do ✂

Before class, photocopy this page, making one for each child.

what children do ✋

Solve the code to find out how a father showed his faith in Jesus in Matthew 9:18.

A–1	C–2	D–3	E–4	H–5	I–6
L–7	M–8	N–9	O–10	P–11	R–12
S–13	T–14	U–15	V–16	W–17	Y–18

__ __ __ __   __ __ __   __ __ __
2 10 8 4   1 9 3   11 15 14

__ __ __ __   __ __ __ __   __ __
18 10 15 12   5 1 9 3   10 9

__ __ __ , __ __ __   __ __ __
5 4 12   1 9 3   13 5 4

__ __ __ __   __ __ __ __ .
17 6 7 7   7 6 16 4

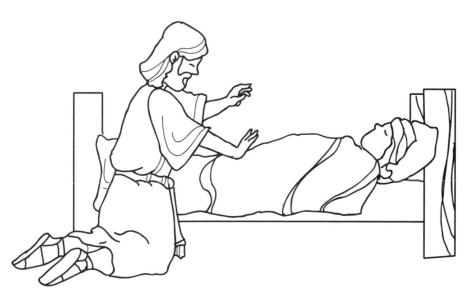

Jesus Heals Jairus's Daughter

Loving Kindness (based on Mark 5:21–43, Luke 8:40–56)

memory verse 📖

Anything is possible if a person believes.
Mark 9:23

discussion questions 💬

1. What did Jairus ask Jesus to do?
2. What did Jesus say Jairus needed to have for his daughter to be healed?

Back to Life

Jairus daughter had died, but Jesus brought her back to life. Look at these pictures. They tell the story. Number the pictures in the order that they happened.

© 2021 Rose Publishing, LLC. Permission to photocopy granted to original purchaser only. *Top 50 Bible Stories about Jesus for Elementary.*

Jesus Teaches about Good Seed

memory verse 📖

Teach them your word, which is truth.
John 17:17

The Four Soils (based on Mark 4:3–20)

Jesus often told people stories so they would understand what he meant. These stories are called parables. Once, Jesus told a parable about a farmer who was planting some seed across his field.

Some of the seed the farmer scattered fell onto a footpath. With nothing to protect it, the birds came and ate the seed. Other seed fell into rocky soil. At first, the seeds sprouted quickly. But it wasn't able to grow deep roots, so it withered away in the hot sun. More seed fell into the weeds and thorns, so it wasn't able to grow any grain.

Finally, some seed fell onto good soil. This seed sprouted, grew, and produced a giant crop, even more than what had been planted!

When Jesus finished the story, he said, "Anyone with ears to hear should listen and understand."

Jesus' disciples were confused, so they asked him to tell him what the parable meant.

Jesus told them that the farmer planting seed is like a person telling others about God.

The seed in the footpath is like people who hear God's message but don't believe.

The seed in rocky soil is like those who believe at first but forget about God when times are hard.

The seed in the weeds and thorns is like people who hear God's word but are more worried about other things.

And the seed that falls on good soil is like people who hear and accept God's word. After they believe, they tell others about God, who then tell even more people. Just like a crop that grows even more than was planted.

discussion questions 💬

1. Why did Jesus speak in parables?
2. What kind of seed does Jesus want us to be?

Good Seed Corn Plant

what you need ✏️

- Yellow and green paper
- Yellow tissue paper
- Wiggle eyes
- Scissors
- Glue
- Crayons or markers

what you do ✂️

Before class, photocopy this page, making one corn ear on yellow paper and four husks on green paper, one set per child.

what children do 🖐️

1. Cut out one ear of corn, four husks, and the Scripture box.
2. Glue two husks on the front and two husks on the back, overlapping on the bottom.
3. Bend down the husks to reveal the corn.
4. Draw a face on the corn.
5. Glue wiggle eyes on the face and tissue paper tassels pointing up from the bottom.
6. Glue the Scripture box to the front of the finished corn.

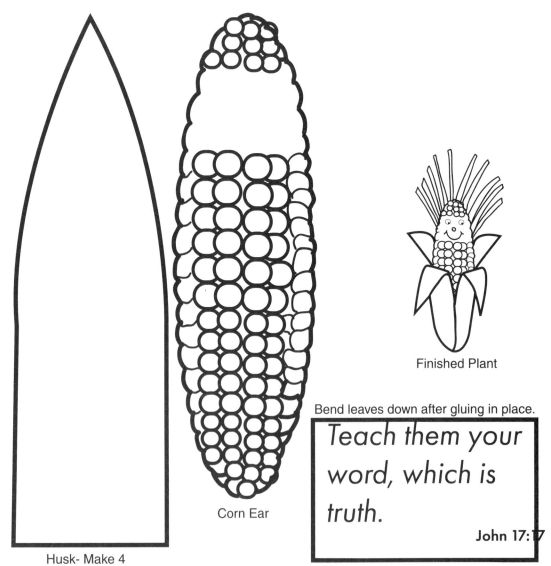

Finished Plant

Husk- Make 4

Corn Ear

Bend leaves down after gluing in place.

> *Teach them your word, which is truth.*
>
> **John 17:17**

What's Wrong With this Farm?

what you need 🖌
....
- Crayons or markers

what you do ✂
....
Before class, photocopy this page, making one for each child.

what children do ✋
....
1. Color the picture.
2. The farm in this picture needs more than good soil to make things right. It is very mixed up, from top to bottom. Circle any mistakes as you color.
3. Turn the page upside down to find the answers.

what's wrong: light bulb plants, baseball sun, weather vane letters, square tractor tires, boy and girl flowers, pig with straight tail, hippo in hay loft, farmer in football uniform holding a football, flag on silo, rug on grass, big leg in barn, compass with wrong letters.

Seed-cret Code

what you need ✎

- Crayons or markers

what you do ✂

Before class, photocopy this page, making one for each child.

what children do ✋

1. Use the code to fill in the blanks below and discover a message about God's Word.

what to say 📢

Jesus told the story of a farmer who scattered seed on his land. It fell in four kinds of places. What were they? Use the code to fill the blanks.

The seed fell:

1. On a H A _ _ _ _ _ _.

    B,2   A,1   D,1   A,3   C,4   A,1   D,3   B,2

2. On __ __ __ __ __ __ __ __ __ __ __

    D,1 C,3 A,2 B,4 D,4   C,4 C,1 A,1 A,2 A,4 D,2

3. Among __ __ __ __ __ __.

    D,3   B,2 C,3 D,1 C,2 D,2

4. In __ __ __ __ __ __ __ __.

   B,1 C,3 C,3 A,3   D,2 C,3 B,3   C,1

Code

	1	2	3	4
A	A	C	D	E
B	G	H	I	K
C	L	N	O	P
D	R	S	T	Y

Jesus Teaches about Good Seed

The Four Soils (based on Mark 5:21–43, Luke 8:40–56)

memory verse 📖

Teach them your word, which is truth.
John 17:17

discussion questions 💬

1. Why did Jesus speak in parables?
2. What kind of seed does Jesus want us to be?

Be The Sower

You can help sow seeds for God. Write names
of people you will tell about God
on the lines below.

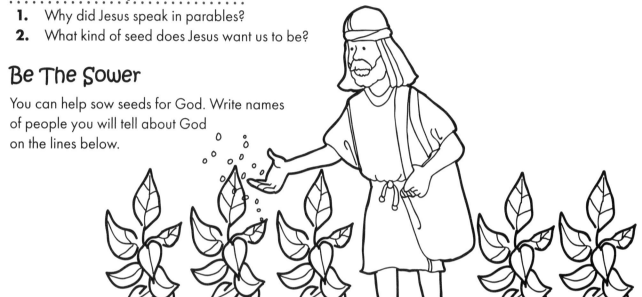

Jesus Teaches about the Best Rule

memory verse 📖

*Love the L*ORD *your God with all your heart, all your soul, all your mind, and all your strength.*
Mark 12:30

Love God, Love Others (based on Mark 12:28–31)

Jesus spent his days on Earth teaching about God, healing people, and forgiving people of their sins. Crowds followed him wherever he went, but not everyone in the crowd liked what he had to say.

Many of the religious leaders and teachers of the time did not like that Jesus said he was God's son. They didn't believe that he was the Savior God had promised. Sometimes, these leaders tried to ask Jesus tricky questions so he would mess up. They thought they could outsmart Jesus, and then people would stop listening to him.

One of these religious leaders asked Jesus one day, "Of all the commandments, which is the most important?"

The man thought Jesus wouldn't be able to answer this question. But for Jesus, it wasn't a problem. Jesus answered by telling the man what God had already said in the Bible.

This is the most important commandment, Jesus said: "'The LORD our God is the one and only LORD. And you must love the Lord your God with all your heart, all your soul, all your mind, and all your strength.' The second is equally important: 'Love your neighbor as yourself.' No other commandment is greater than these."

discussion questions 💬

1. Why did some people want to trick Jesus?
2. What did Jesus say were the most important commandments?

Heart Weaving

what you need ✏

- Red and white paper
- Scissors
- Tape

what you do ✂

Before class, photocopy this page on red and white, making one of each color for each child.

what children do ✋

1. Follow the instructions in the diagram below to make a woven heart.

what to say 📢

Jesus wants us to serve him and care about others because we love him so much. Jesus even said that our loving attitudes would show others that we are his disciples. Our hearts will be joined together in love when we follow Jesus' commandment.

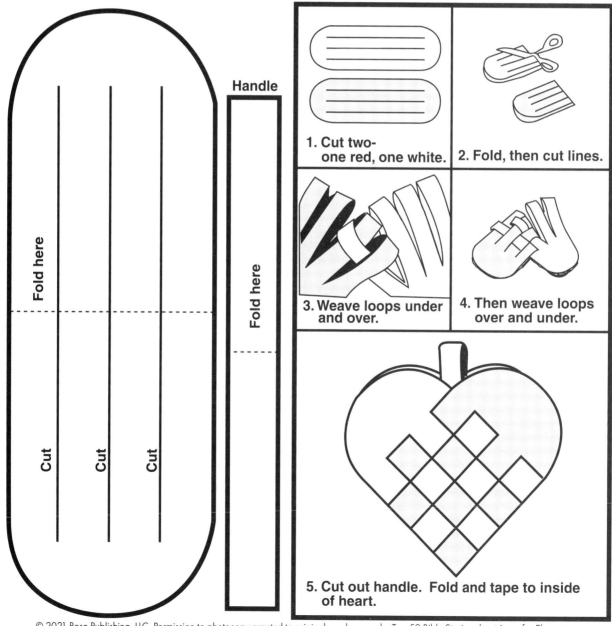

Handle

Fold here

Fold here

Cut

Cut

Cut

1. Cut two— one red, one white.

2. Fold, then cut lines.

3. Weave loops under and over.

4. Then weave loops over and under.

5. Cut out handle. Fold and tape to inside of heart.

Love One Another Quiz

what you need ✎

- Crayons or markers

what you do ✂

Before class, photocopy this page, making one for each child.

what children do ✋

1. Read the following sentences.
2. Color the heart beside each sentence that shows obedience to Jesus' command.
3. Rewrite the sentences that show disobedience to Jesus' command. Change them to show love.

what to say 📢

People in the Old Testament lived under the Old Testament law. Because of Jesus, we live in God's grace, so we want to keep his law. We love because we are loved.

♡ **1.** You can borrow my bike this week.

♡ **2.** I'll rake leaves for you.

♡ **3.** Who asked for your advice?

♡ **4.** Your new outfit looks great!

♡ **5.** Who needs you for a friend?

♡ **6.** Do you want some help on your homework?

♡ **7.** I'm glad I met you.

♡ **8.** How can you be so stupid?

♡ **9.** Let's go to church together.

♡ **10.** You are too ugly for words.

♡ **11.** Don't speak to me ever again.

♡ **12.** I promise to pray for you.

Stained Glass Message

what you need ✏️

- Crayons or markers

what you do ✂️

Before class, photocopy this page, making one for each child.

what children do ✋

1. Color the sections with a dot red to find the secret for obeying God's best rule of all.
2. Color the other sections as you like.

what to say 📣

When we put God and others first, we love as Jesus did.

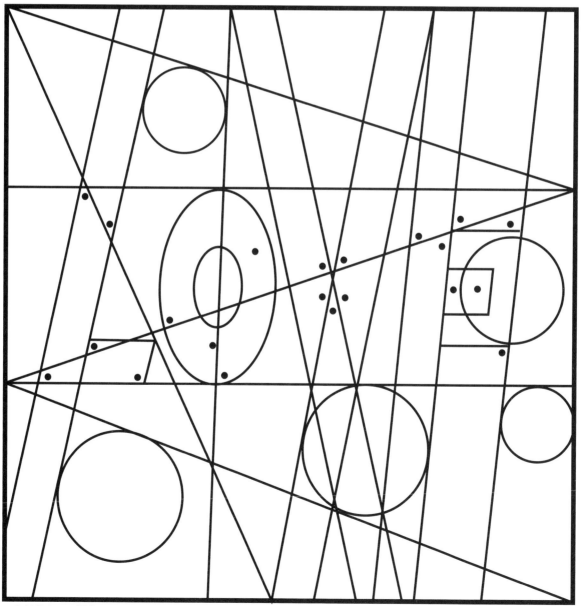

Jesus Teaches about the Best Rule

Love God, Love Others (based on Mark 12:28–31)

memory verse 📖

Love the LORD your God with all your heart, all your soul, all your mind, and all your strength.
Mark 12:30

discussion questions 💬

Finished Tube Person

1. Why did some people want to trick Jesus?
2. What did Jesus say were the most important commandments?

Love God Tube People

1. Cut toilet-paper or paper-towel tubes to 4-inch lengths.
2. Color and cut out each piece.
3. Snip lines on hair to create fringe.
4. Glue the body wrap around the tube.
5. Glue the hair on top.
6. Glue legs to the base and arms on each side.

Hair

Arm

Arm

Legs

I can love God. (Mark 12:28–31)

Jesus Feeds 5,000

memory verse 📖

God who takes care of me will supply all your needs from his glorious riches, which have been given to us in Christ Jesus.
Philippians 4:19

A Boy Shares His Lunch (based on John 6:5–14)

One day, Jesus was preaching to a large crowd. The people had been listening all morning, and when lunchtime came, Jesus wanted to feed them.

Jesus asked Philip, his disciple, "Where can we buy bread to feed all these people?"

Philip told Jesus it was impossible to feed all the people who had gathered. But Jesus knew that wasn't true.

Another disciple said, "There's a young boy here with five barley loaves and two fish." But what good would that do?

Jesus asked the crowd to sit down. There were more than 5,000 people! Then Jesus took the loaves and fish, gave thanks to God, and gave the food to the people.

When everyone ate what they wanted, Jesus' asked his disciples to collect the leftovers. They filled twelve baskets with leftovers. How was this possible, when there were only five loaves and two fish?

It was a miracle! The people exclaimed, "Surely, he is the Prophet we have been expecting!"

discussion questions 💬

1. What food did the boy have to share?
2. How was there enough food to feed all the people?

Mixed Up Story

what you need 🖌

- Bibles
- Crayons or markers

what you do ✂

Before class, photocopy this page, making one for each child.

what children do ✋

1. Unscramble the words and fill in the blanks to read about Jesus' miracle. Hint: Most of the words are numbers.

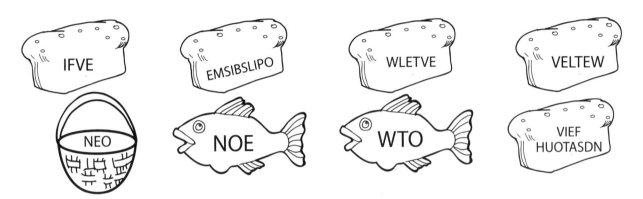

A great crowd followed Jesus. When they became hungry, Jesus asked

his disciples where they could buy food. Philip answered that it was

_____. Jesus knew that _____ small boy

would supply the food. The food was _____ loaves of

bread and _____ fish. Jesus asked the people to sit down.

He blessed the food and fed over _____ people with it.

When everyone was full, the _____ disciples picked up

over _____ baskets of leftover food. The people knew that

Jesus was the _____ whom God had promised to send.

A Boy Shared His Lunch

what you need ✎

- Crayons or markers
- Scissors
- Glue
- Construction paper
- Hole punch
- Paper fastener

what you do ✂

Before class, photocopy this page, making one for each child.

what children do 🖐

1. Color the picture.
2. Cut out Jesus, the boy, and the boy's arm.
3. Glue Jesus and the boy onto construction paper.
4. Punch a hole through both black dots.
5. Attach the arm to the body with a paper fastener.
6. Move the boy's arm up as he shares his lunch with Jesus.

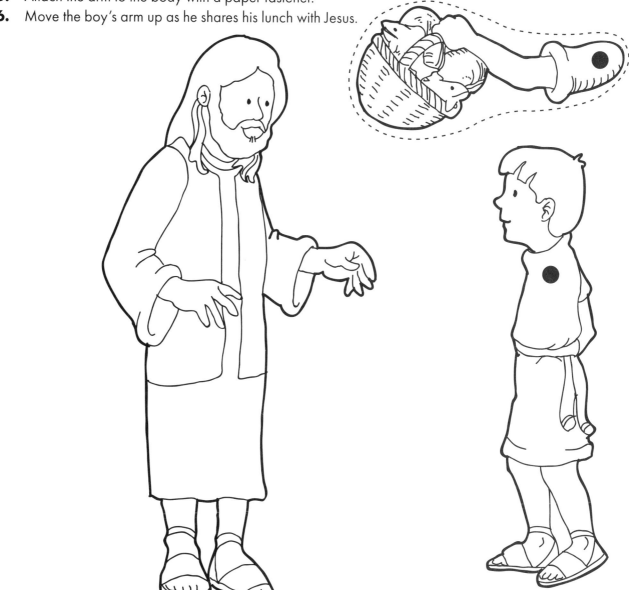

I Can Share . . .

what you need ✎

- Crayons or markers

what you do ✂

Before class, photocopy this page, making one for each child.

what children do ✋

1. Read the sentences below. Draw a line from each sentence to the picture that matches it.
2. Draw something that you can share with someone else this week in the empty box.

what to say 📢

The little boy who shared his lunch had no idea how many people he would help. He was glad to share what he had, even though it seemed very small. Sharing is something each of us can do. Sharing is a way to show that we care about others.

1. I can share my toys.

2. I can share my friends.

3. I can share my home and family.

4. I can share my faith in God.

Draw something you can share this week.

I can share:

Jesus Feeds 5,000

A Boy Shares His Lunch (based on John 6:5–14)

memory verse 📖

God who takes care of me will supply all your needs from his glorious riches, which have been given to us in Christ Jesus.
Philippians 4:19

discussion questions 💬

1. What food did the boy have to share?
2. How was there enough food to feed all the people?

Find the Loaves and Fish

Five loaves, two fish, a cross, a Bible, an apple, a snake and a sheep are hidden in the picture below.

1. Color the picture.
2. When you find the hidden pictures, make a small pencil dot on the objects you find.
3. Erase the marks and ask someone else to find them.

Jesus Walks on Water

memory verse 📖

Don't be afraid. I am here to help you.

Isaiah 41:13

One Scary, Stormy Night (based on Matthew 14:22–36)

One evening, Jesus sent his disciples away in a boat to cross a lake. Jesus stayed on the shore to pray.

When night fell, a storm came, and the disciples were in trouble. Waves rocked the boat, and a strong wind roared overhead.

Just when they started to worry, the disciples saw Jesus. He was walking on the water! At first, the disciples thought Jesus was a ghost. They were terrified.

"Don't be afraid," Jesus said. "Take courage. I am here!"

Peter, one of Jesus' disciples, said, "Lord, if it's really you, tell me to come to you." So Jesus told him to come.

At first, Peter was amazed. He, too, was walking on water! But when he looked down, he was afraid and began to sink.

Jesus grabbed Peter by the hand. "You have so little faith," Jesus said. "Why did you doubt me."

When they returned to the boat, the disciples were amazed and worshiped Jesus. He truly was the Son of God.

discussion questions 💬

1. What did Jesus tell the disciples when they were scared?
2. Why did Peter start to sink when he was afraid?

What Did They Say?

what you need ✎

- Crayons or markers

what you do ✂

Before class, photocopy this page, making one for each child.

what children do ✋

1. Cross out every other letter, beginning with "G" to find out what the disciples said after they saw Jesus walk on water.
2. Color the picture.

G̶ T X R A U R L Q Y K Y C O W U
L A S R T E P T D H C E
F S I O J N M O B F Z G I O N D.

___ ___ ___ ___ ___ ___   ___ ___ ___   ___ ___ ___ ___

___ ___ ___   ___ ___   ___ ___ ___ ___

Flip-Flap Story

what you need ✎

- Scissors
- Tape
- Crayons or markers

what you do ✂

Before class, photocopy this page, making one for each child.

what children do ✋

1. Cut the pattern on the solid lines.
2. Tape the flap to the edge so that the picture is facing forward.
3. Flip the flap back and forth to tell the story.
4. Color the picture.

Safe Sailing

what you need ✎

- Card stock
- Scissors
- Tissue paper in various shades of blue
- Hole punch
- Clear Con-Tact paper

what you do ✄

Before class, photocopy this page onto card stock, making one for each child. Cut various shades of blue tissue paper into small sections.

what children do 🖐

1. Cut out the boat.
2. Cut out the center of the sail. Use a hole punch to get started.
3. Press the sailboat onto a sheet of clear Con-Tact paper.
4. Press blue tissue paper around the boat for water.
5. Cover the back with another sheet of clear Con-Tact paper.

Matthew 14:22-36

Jesus Walks on Water

One Scary, Stormy Night (based on Matthew 14:22–36)

memory verse 📖

Don't be afraid. I am here to help you.

Isaiah 41:13

discussion questions 💬

1. What did Jesus tell the disciples when they were scared?
2. Why did Peter start to sink when he was afraid?

Walked on Water Word Search

Find the words from this week's story in the word search.

DISCIPLES	SINK	JESUS	HAND
GHOST	WIND	COURAGE	ALONE
AFRAID	HIMSELF	REACHED	TERRIFIED
FAITH	NIGHT	EVENING	CAUGHT
BOAT	SAVE	WALKING	
FEAR	PRAY	PETER	

```
T W I N D N F V N I G H T Z W
A I N P E Q W T O J F F Z L A
F B B Y U Y N Q B T P E Z B L
R O T E R R I F I E D A H S K
A A J V I T E I D H O R M P I
I T E U F X U Q D R N J S E N
D I S C I P L E S G H O S T G
F I U K A C C K I P I H B E C
E Q S Z Y E A C N R M G R R P
R R F M L V U O K A S K F U K
U N A C A E G U O Y E E J A E
H S I T L N H R E I L Q L S B
A B T N O I T A Y Q F X G A L
N W H P N N B G E J A I Y V X
D N F Y E G R E A C H E D E K
```

Listening to Jesus

memory verse

Get all the advice and instruction you can, so you will be wise the rest of your life.
Proverbs 19:20

Mary Listens (based on Luke 10:38–42)

Mary and Martha were sisters. They also had a brother named Lazarus. Jesus was one of their very good friends, and he visited them often.

One day, Jesus visited Mary and Martha with his disciples. Mary and Martha were so excited to have their friend Jesus in their home. However, they had different ideas on how to welcome him.

Mary wanted to hear everything Jesus had to say. She sat at Jesus' feet, listening to him as he taught about God.

Martha wanted to host a big dinner for Jesus. While Jesus taught, Martha was busy cooking and preparing for the meal. She didn't have time to hear anything he had to say! Martha started to get frustrated with her sister, Mary, for not helping.

"Lord," Martha asked Jesus, "doesn't it seem unfair to you that my sister just sits here while I do all the work? Tell her to come and help me."

Jesus looked at Martha. "My dear Martha," Jesus responded, "you are worried and upset over all these details! There is only one thing worth being concerned about. Mary has discovered it."

What do you think that was? Jesus was telling Martha that Mary knew it was important to listen to Jesus.

Because of Jesus, we don't have to work for God's love. We just have to show Jesus we love him by listening to him.

discussion questions

1. Why was Martha upset with Mary?
2. How did Jesus respond to Martha?

Scene-It News

what you need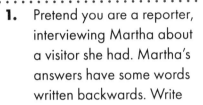

- Pencils

what you do ✄

Before class, photocopy this page, making one for each child.

what children do ✋

1. Pretend you are a reporter, interviewing Martha about a visitor she had. Martha's answers have some words written backwards. Write them correctly in the blanks.

Reporter: Martha, who lives in your house with you?

Martha: My sister, (yraM), and my brother (surazaL).

_____, _____

Reporter: What special visitors came to see you?

Martha: (suseJ) and his (selpicsid).

_____, _____

Reporter: What did you do?

Martha: I (dekooc) and (dekab) and (denaelc esuoh)

_____, _____, _____

Reporter: What did Mary do?

Martha: She (tas) at Jesus' (teef), listening to him. I said, "Lord, don't you (erac) that she has left me to do all the (krow)?"

_____, _____, _____, _____

Reporter: What did Jesus say?

Martha: He said, "I was (deirrow) and (tespu) about many (sgniht), but only (eno) thing was needed, and (yraM) had (nesohc) what is (retteb)."

_____, _____, _____, _____

_____, _____, _____

House of Honor

what you need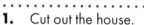

- Scissors
- Crayons or markers
- Decorative materials
- Glue
- Magnet

what you do ✂

Before class, photocopy this page, making one for each child.

what children do 🖐

1. Cut out the house.
2. Color and decorate the house.
3. Glue a magnet to the back of the house.
4. Display the magnet in your home as a reminder to honor Jesus.

what to say 📢

How did Mary honor Jesus? She stopped and listened to him. Place this magnet in your home so you remember to stop and listen to Jesus, too.

Listen Up Crossword

what you need ✐

- Crayons or markers

what you do ✂

Before class, photocopy this page, making one for each child.

what children do ✋

1. Fit the words from this week's story in the crossword.
2. Count the number of letters in each word and write it beside the word.
3. Put the longest words in the crossword first. Then move to the next longest word.

what to say 📢

Mary and Martha had two different responses. Martha was too busy cooking and cleaning to listen to Jesus. But Mary honored Jesus by listening to him.

PREPARATIONS   OPENED

DISTRACTED   SISTER

DISCIPLES   HOUSE

LISTENING   JESUS

VILLAGE   UPSET

WORRIED   WOMAN

BETTER   FEET

MARTHA   MARY

MYSELF   WORK

Listening to Jesus

Mary Listens (based on Luke 10:38–42)

memory verse

Get all the advice and instruction you can, so you will be wise the rest of your life.
Proverbs 19:20

discussion questions

1. Why was Martha upset with Mary?
2. How did Jesus respond to Martha?

Time to Listen

You can listen to God when you pray. Make this sign as a reminder to pray often.

1. Draw a picture of yourself praying on the left side of the prayer sign.
2. Color and cut out the prayer sign.
3. Decorate craft sticks with markers, stickers, or other decorative items.
4. Glue the sticks together to form a square.
5. Glue the prayer sign to the back of the craft sticks.
6. Tie yarn to the top left and right sides of the square to make a hanger.

Jesus & Money from a Fish

memory verse 📖

God is with those who obey him.
Psalm 14:5

Fishy Money (based on Matthew 17:24–27)

In Bible times, people had to pay something called a Temple tax. The Temple tax helped keep the Temple running, so people could go there to worship God.

One day, Jesus and his disciples were visiting a city. When they arrived, a man came to Peter and asked him, "Doesn't your teacher pay the Temple tax?"

Peter nodded his head yes. Of course Jesus paid the Temple tax! There was only one problem—Peter didn't have any money.

Peter went into the house where they were staying to ask Jesus where he could get some money for the Temple tax. Peter was surprised when he heard what Jesus said.

"Go down to the lake and throw in a line," Jesus said. "Open the mouth of the first fish you catch, and you will find a large silver coin. Take it and pay the tax for both of us."

Peter went to the lake, and it happened just as Jesus said it would. There was a silver coin in the first fish he caught! Peter continued to the Temple to pay the tax. He was so thankful that his Savior provided for him.

Jesus has paid the price for all of us. Because of Jesus, we can have eternal life with God. All we have to do is believe and obey, just like Peter did in this story.

discussion

questions 💬

1. Who did Peter talk to when he needed something?
2. How has Jesus provided for you?

A Fishy Surprise

what you need ✎

- Crayons or markers
- Scissors
- Clear Con-Tact paper
- Pennies, one per child

what you do ✂

Before class, photocopy this page, making one for each child.

what children do ✋

1. Color both fish and cut them out.
2. Center the front fish onto clear Con-Tact paper, face-down. Place a penny in the middle of the open mouth.
3. Glue the back fish to the front fish.
4. Cover the back with Con-Tact paper.

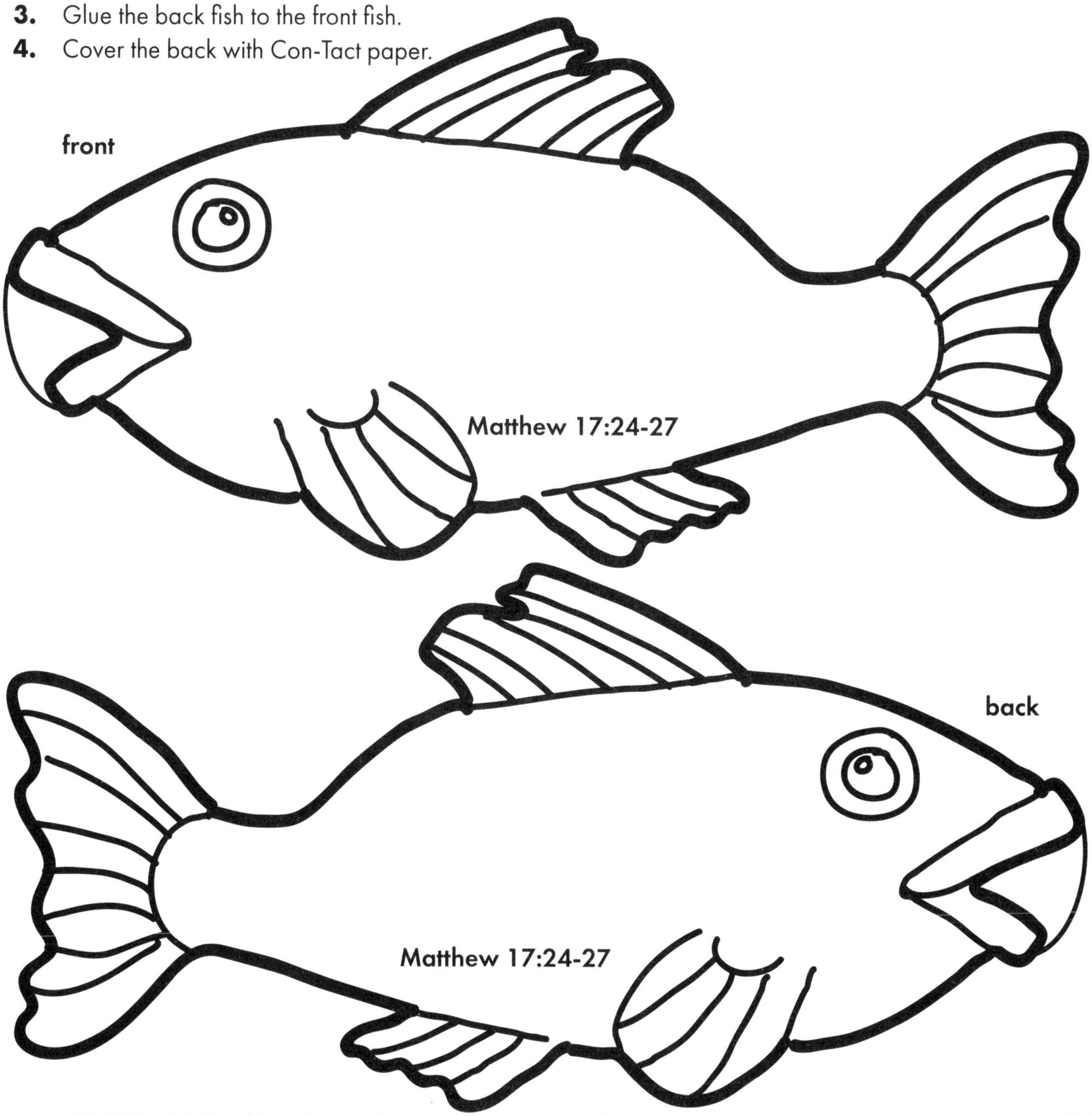

front

Matthew 17:24-27

back

Matthew 17:24-27

A Bank for God

what you need 🖌

- Crayons or markers
- Scissors
- Glue
- Empty chip can, one per child

what you do ✂

Before class, photocopy this page, making one for each child.

what children do ✋

1. Color and cut out the bank wrap.
2. Glue the wrap to a chip can.
3. Collect your tithes in the can.

My Tithes and Offerings

Hidden Penny

what you need ✎

- Crayons or markers
- Scissors
- Glue
- Construction paper
- Pennies, one for each child

what you do ✂

Before class, photocopy this page, making one for each child.

what children do ✋

1. Color and cut out the fish.
2. Fold on the dashed line.
3. Glue the fish to a sheet of construction paper.
4. Put some glue along the fold line, but not under the face portion of the fish so it can flap open.
5. Glue a penny under the face portion of the fish.

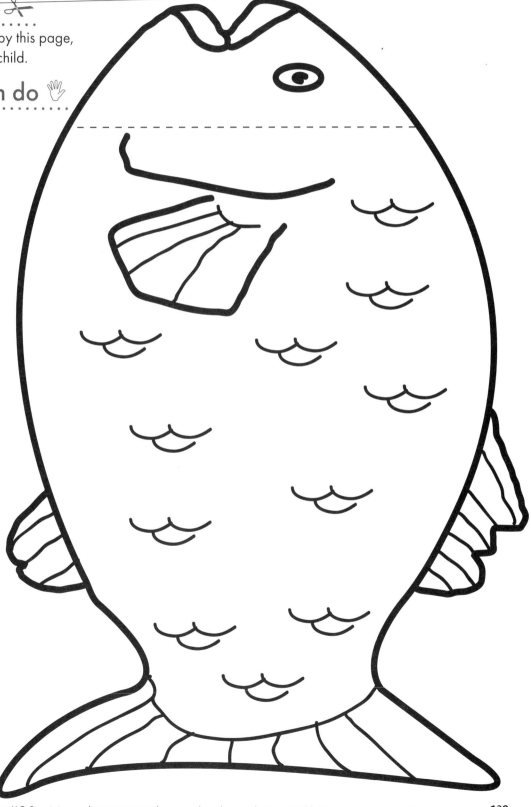

Jesus & Money from a Fish

Fishy Money (based on Matthew 17:24–27)

memory verse 📖

God is with those who obey him.

Psalm 14:5

discussion questions 💬

1. Who did Peter talk to when he needed something?
2. How has Jesus provided for you?

Obedience Reminder

Peter might have thought that Jesus' instructions were strange, but he obeyed anyway. You can obey Jesus, too, by reading God's Word.

1. Color each item according to the label next to it.
2. Cut out each item.
3. Glue the sun to the top of the bookmark.
4. Glue the tulip and stem on top of the sun.
5. Use a marker to write the memory verse near the bottom of the bookmark.
6. Draw a thick zig-zag line from the sun down to the words.

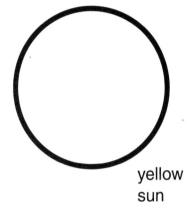

yellow sun

red tulip

green stem

blue bookmark

Jesus Teaches about the Good Samaritan

memory verse 📖

Love each other.
John 15:17

Unexpected Help (based on Luke 10:25–37)

Jesus taught others about God by telling stories, also known as parables. One story he told is called the Parable of the Good Samaritan.

A Jewish man was traveling one day to a nearby city. He was walking down a road when a group of bandits attacked him! The bandits beat the man, robbed him, and left him for dead on the side of the road.

Soon, a priest walked by. *Maybe this priest will help me*, the dying man thought. However, when the priest saw the man, he crossed to the other side of the road and kept going.

Then, a Temple assistant passed by. The Temple assistant didn't help, either! He looked at the man lying on the ground but kept walking.

Finally, a Samaritan man walked by. In Bible times, Samaritan and Jewish people hated each other. The dying man never thought the Samaritan would help him. But, Jesus said the Samaritan felt compassion for the dying man. The Samaritan took care of his wounds and bandaged him and then took him to an inn to be taken care of.

When he finished the story, Jesus said that we should show love and mercy to everyone, no matter who they are, just like the Samaritan did.

discussion questions 💬

1. Why was the dying man surprised the Samaritan cared for him?
2. How can you help others like the Good Samaritan helped the dying man?

First Aid Helpers

what you need 🖌

- Fabric scraps
- Glue
- Crayons or markers
- Scissors

what you do ✂

Before class, photocopy this page, making one for each child. Cut fabric scraps into small strips.

what children do ✋

1. Make an arm sling to tie around the hurt man's neck by gluing a piece of fabric onto the sling.
2. Place clean bandages on his head and knee by gluing fabric onto the hurt man's head and knee.
3. Color the rest of the picture.

what to say 📢

The Good Samaritan wrapped soft, clean bandages on the man's cuts. Then he took him to an inn where he could get well again. Jesus said we should follow the Good Samaritan's example. He wants us to care for those who need help. You can practice by giving first aid to this hurt man.

Find the Good Samaritans

what you need 🖌

- Crayons or markers
- Scissors
- Glue
- Card stock
- Hole punch
- Paper fastener

what you do ✂

Before class, photocopy this page, making one for each child.

what children do ✋

1. Draw a circle around the children who are helping; color the children who are not helping.
2. Cut out the arrow and glue it to card stock for support. Cut out the arrow again.
3. Punch a hole on the black dot and attach the arrow with a paper fastener.
4. Glue this page onto card stock.
5. Take turns spinning the arrow with a friend and describe the helpful or hurtful things taking place in each picture you land on.

A Good Neighbor

what you need 🖌

- Pencils
- Crayons or markers

what you do ✂

Before class, photocopy this page, making one for each child.

what children do 🖐

1. Pick one of these people in need.
2. Write a story of how you could be a good neighbor.
3. Color the pictures.

I can be a good neighbor by...

_____

_____

_____

_____

_____

_____

_____

_____

_____

_____

_____

_____

_____

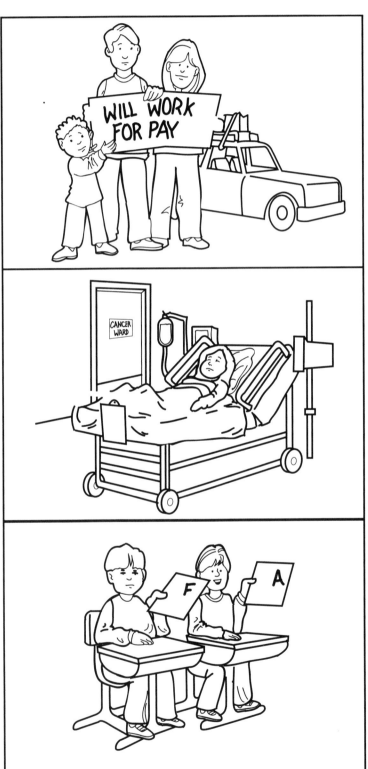

Jesus Teaches about the Good Samaritan

Unexpected Help (based on Luke 10:25–37)

memory verse 📖

Love each other.
John 15:17

discussion questions 💬

1. Why was the dying man surprised the Samaritan cared for him?
2. How can you help others like the Good Samaritan helped the dying man?

Tell The Story

1. Color and cut out the figures.
2. Use the figures to tell the story about the Good Samaritan to a friend or family member.

Jesus Teaches about Prayer

memory verse 📖

Never stop praying.
1 Thessalonians 5:17

The Lord's Prayer (based on Luke 11:1–10)

Jesus' disciples once asked him, "Lord teach us to pray."

Jesus was glad they asked. He knew it was part of his reason for being on Earth—to help others know more about God. Jesus said, "This is how you should pray," he said.

> Father, may your name be kept holy.
> May your Kingdom come soon.
> Give us each day the food we need,
> and forgive us our sins,
> as we forgive those who sin against us.
> And don't let us yield to temptation."

Jesus gave them a prayer as an example. And this prayer is one we can say any time! It's called "The Lord's Prayer," because our Lord Jesus prayed it.

But Jesus didn't stop there. Jesus told us that if we need something, we should keep asking God for it, even if he doesn't answer at first. He told a story about a man who knocked on his friend's door one night, asking to borrow some bread. At first, the friend said no. But Jesus said if the man would keep knocking and keep asking, the friend would eventually give the man what he needed.

Jesus said, "Everyone who asks, receives. Everyone who seeks, finds. And to everyone who knocks, the door will be opened."

God wants us to talk to him like a friend. We can ask him for anything we need, trusting that God will provide for us.

discussion questions 💬

1. What is the name of the prayer Jesus prayed?
2. What can you ask God for? Is there something you need?

Ask, Seek, Knock Door

what you need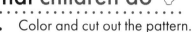

- Crayons or markers
- Scissors
- Rulers, one for each child
- Colored paper
- Glue

Finished Door

what you do ✂

Before class, photocopy this page, making one for each child. Make a sample to demonstrate.

what children do ✋

1. Color and cut out the pattern.
2. Fold the pattern in half and cut the doors on the solid lines; unfold the pattern.
3. Draw a need you have in the center of a colored piece of paper to fill a 4-inch space.
4. Fold the colored paper inward ½-inch on both sides, and then ½-inch more.
5. Unfold and glue the edges of the pattern on top of the paper.

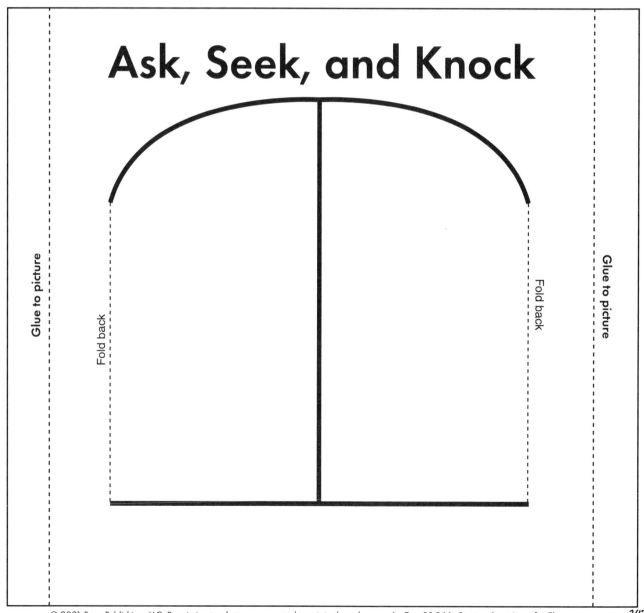

Ask, Seek, and Knock

Glue to picture

Fold back

Fold back

Glue to picture

Prayer Quiz

what you need ✎

- Crayons or markers

what you do ✂

Before class, photocopy this page, making one for each child.

what children do ✋

1. Read the sentences below. Draw a circle around each correct answer in the parenthesis.

what to say 📢

Prayer is important in our lives today, just as it was for Jesus. God hears and answers us when we talk to him. He asks us to bring our joys as well as our problems to him in prayer.

1. The disciples wanted Jesus to teach them to (pray) (fish).

2. The prayer Jesus taught them is called the (Lord's prayer) (disciples' prayer).

3. The prayer Jesus taught them teaches us to (praise God first) (just ask for something and say "Amen" since God is so busy).

4. Jesus said to ask for (a year's worth of requests so we won't bother God so often) (daily needs just as we ask of our parents).

5. Jesus also taught that we should ask God for (forgiveness if we have done wrong) (ways to get even with mean people).

6. We are to ask God to help us (say "no" to wrong things) (put down people if they are doing wrong things).

7. Jesus compared our coming to God in prayer with (a sick person asking a doctor for medicine) (a stranger asking for food).

8. Jesus tells us to ask for (forgiveness) (X-ray vision).

9. The three words Jesus used to describe how to pray were (pray, praise and promises) (ask, seek and knock).

10. Jesus said that if we ask, seek and knock, God will (put it on his list to think about) (answer our prayers).

Pray Like Jesus

what you need

- Crayons or markers.

what you do ✂

Before class, photocopy this page, making one for each child.

what children do ✋

1. Color the picture of Jesus.
2. In the thought bubble, write a prayer to Jesus based on the Lord's Prayer.
3. Draw yourself next to the thought balloon.

Jesus Teaches about Prayer

The Lord's Prayer (based on Luke 11:1–10)

memory verse 📖

Never stop praying.
1 Thessalonians 5:17

discussion questions 💬

1. What is the name of the prayer Jesus prayed?
2. What can you ask God for? Is there something you need?

A Rebus Story

Can you read the story below using the pictures? Take turns reading it with a friend. You can read the words while your friend "reads" the pictures. Then do it the opposite way.

1 day 2 men went to the [temple] to [pray]. The Pharisee stood and prayed, "God, thank you that [I] am not like other men. [I] fast twice in the week. [I] give tithes of all my [money] and what I possess." But the tax collector stood with his [head] bowed. He said, "God, 4 give my sins." [Jesus] said, "The tax collector received the clean [heart]."

Jesus & the Rich Young Ruler

memory verse 📖

Wherever your treasure is, there the desires of your heart will also be.
Luke 12:34

Love God, Not Money (based on Mark 10:17–22)

People often came to Jesus asking for wisdom or advice. This happened one day as Jesus was making his way to Jerusalem. A rich young ruler stopped him and asked, "Good Teacher, what must I do to inherit eternal life."

At first, Jesus answered by telling the man to follow the Ten Commandments: "You must not murder. You must not commit adultery. You must not steal. You must not testify falsely. You must not cheat anyone. Honor your father and mother."

Jesus knew everything about this man. He knew the man's heart and what was most important to him. So Jesus was not surprised by the rich young ruler's response.

"Teacher," he said, "I've obeyed all these commandments since I was young."

Jesus knew this was true. But he also knew there was something the man had not done. Even though the man followed all the laws, Jesus knew that the man didn't love God with all his heart. That's why Jesus said, "Go and sell all of your possessions and give the money to the poor."

The rich young ruler was surprised. He loved his money—it was very important to him. He didn't know if he could make that kind of sacrifice.

Looking away from Jesus, the man frowned and walked away sad. Jesus was sad, too. He loved the rich young ruler. But the man loved his things too much.

You might not have a lot of things, but you can still give what you have to God.

discussion questions 💬

1. Why was the rich young ruler sad at the end of the story?
2. What are some things you can give for Jesus?

Give What You Have Mobile

what you need ✏️

- Crayons or markers
- Scissors
- Hole punch
- String
- Glue

what you do ✂️

Before class, photocopy this page, making one for each child. Make a sample to demonstrate.

what children do ✋

1. Color and cut out the mobile on the solid lines.
2. Punch a hole in the mobile on the black dot and insert a string for hanging.
3. Fold the mobiles on the dashed lines to form a diamond shape.
4. Glue the tabs under the corresponding panels.

what to say 📢

Jesus wants us to give what we have. Some people, like the rich young ruler, have a lot that they might not want to give up. You might not have money, but you still have a lot to give. Make this mobile so you can remember to give what you have.

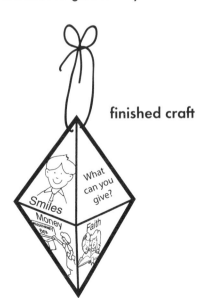

finished craft

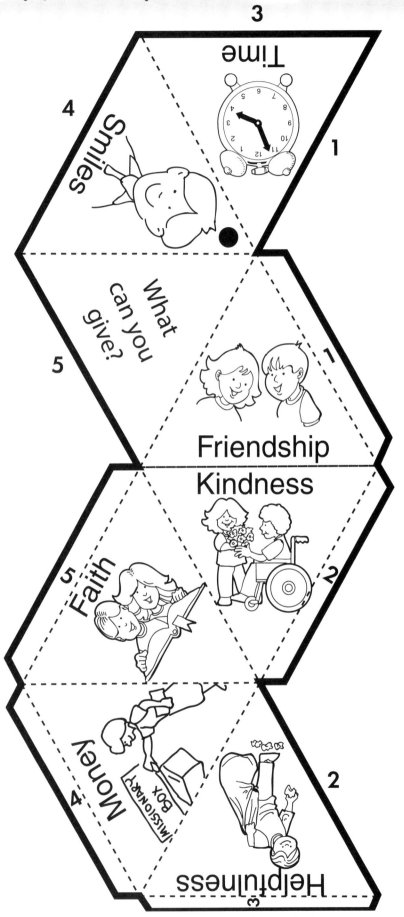

Bell Pull Reminder

what you need

- Colored poster board
- Scissors
- Crayons or markers
- Jumbo craft sticks, one for each child
- Glue
- Yarn
- Hole punch
- Jingle bells

what you do ✂

Before class, photocopy this page onto colored poster board, making one for each child. Make a sample to demonstrate. Cut yarn into 6-inch lengths, making two for each child.

what children do ✋

1. Cut out number one and decorate with crayons or markers.
2. Glue craft stick to back of the one.
3. Tie yarn to the end of the craft stick to make a bow.
4. Punch hole on bottom of number one where indicated.
5. Tie yarn to the jingle bell. Loop yarn through hole at the bottom of the one and tie to secure.

what to say 📢

The rich young man wanted to put his money before Jesus and still get to Heaven. Is money sinful? No, it is only sinful when it becomes more important than God. So be careful of your possessions. Every time you hear the bell from this craft you will be reminded to keep Jesus first.

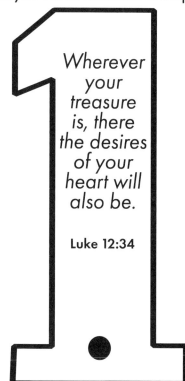

Wherever your treasure is, there the desires of your heart will also be.

Luke 12:34

Change Holder

what you need ✎

- Colored poster board
- Crayons or markers
- Craft sticks
- Hairspray can lids
- Scissors
- Glue
- Small stickers of Jesus

what you do ✄

Before class, photocopy this page onto colored poster board, making one for each child. Make a sample to demonstrate. Give each child a verse square.

what children do ✋

1. Color and cut out verse square.
2. Glue craft sticks together to form a square.
3. Glue the verse square to the back of the craft sticks.
4. Glue a lid on the square. This will hold your change.
5. Place stickers of Jesus on the square and encourage them to draw hearts around Jesus.

what to say 📢

This Change Holder will be a good place for you to keep your money. When you see Jesus inside the hearts, remember the rich, young man who came to see Jesus. Keep Jesus first in your heart.

Wherever your treasure is, there the desires of your heart will also be.

Luke 12:34

Jesus & the Rich Young Ruler

Love God, Not Money (based on Mark 10:17–22)

memory verse 📖

Wherever your treasure is, there the desires of your heart will also be.
Luke 12:34

discussion questions 💬

1. Why was the rich young ruler sad at the end of the story?
2. What are some things you can give for Jesus?

The Path to Heaven

The rich young man wanted to reach Heaven. There was just one thing standing in his way. What did he choose instead? Complete the maze to find out.

The Kingdom of God

memory verse

Seek the Kingdom of God above all else.
Matthew 6:33

Everything Is Possible with God (based on Mark 10:23–31)

A rich man once asked Jesus how he could enter the Kingdom of God. The Kingdom of God means two things. The Kingdom of God is Heaven, but it is also everyone on Earth who believes in Jesus.

First, Jesus told him to follow all the commands in the Old Testament. When the man said he had done this, Jesus told him to sell all his possessions. The rich man loved his possessions and did not want to sell them, so he walked away very sad.

After the rich man left, Jesus said to his disciples, "Dear children, it is very hard to enter the Kingdom of God."

At first, Jesus' disciples were confused. They asked Jesus, "Then who in the world can be saved?"

"Humanly speaking, it is impossible," Jesus said. "But not with God. Everything is possible with God."

Peter, one of Jesus' disciples, told Jesus that they had given everything up to follow him. Would this be enough?

Jesus said, "Yes." Anyone who gives up what's important to them to share the Good News will have a hundred times more in the Kingdom of God. They will live forever with him in Heaven!

Jesus wants us to know that everything we have is already his. That's why we can give those things up and follow him. Showing love to others helps build God's Kingdom!

discussion questions

1. What is the Kingdom of God?
2. What is something you can give up to follow Jesus?

Clothes Basket Relay

what you need

- Several articles of clothing
- Laundry baskets, one for each team

what you do ✂

In the weeks before playing this game, ask people in church to bring their cast-off clothing such as oversized T-shirts, hats, scarves, shoes, aprons, gym shorts, etc.

Set up laundry baskets at one end of the playing area. Fill each basket with five to seven articles of clothing.

what children do 🖐

1. Divide into teams of four or five kids.
2. One player from each team runs across the playing area to put on an article of clothing from the basket.
3. Player says, "Seek the Kingdom of God above all else!" and returns to their team still wearing the item.
4. Player tags the next team member in line.
5. The first team to complete the race and put on some new clothing says the verse aloud.

what to say 📣

That was a pretty fun game! Sometimes it seems like the clothes we wear are really important, but God says that doing the right thing and telling other people about God is even more important than wearing the latest and greatest clothing. Let's say the verse all together a few more times.

Jesus Teaches about Heaven

what you need

- Crayons or markers
- Scissors
- Glue
- Cardboard
- Straight pins
- Yellow yarn or string

what you do ✄

Before class, photocopy this page, making one for each child.

what children do ✋

1. Color the picture of Heaven and cut it out on the outside border.
2. Glue the picture to a piece of cardboard.
3. Push straight pins into the cardboard, through each of the dots.
4. Wind yellow string or yarn around the pin at one. Continue winding the string around each pin in numerical order, finishing back at number one. It should look like a crown.

what to say 📢

Those who love God more than anything will get crowns in Heaven!

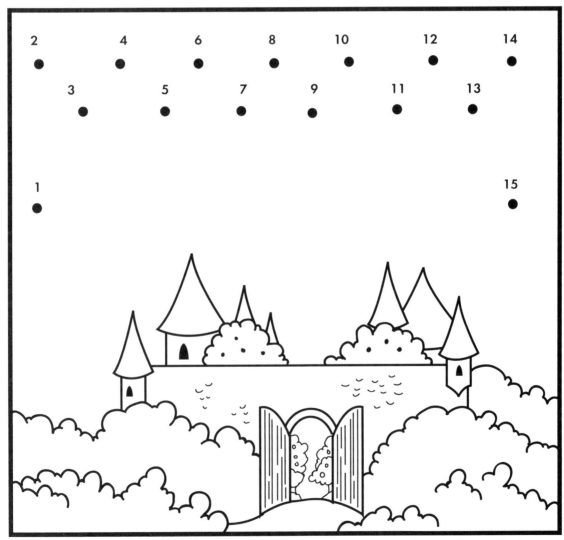

High in the Sky

what you need ✎

- Scissors
- ¼-inch ribbon
- Ruler
- Plastic straws, one for each child
- Colored paper
- Black markers
- Glue
- Clear tape

what you do ✂

Before class, photocopy this page, making one for each child. Cut ribbon into 4-, 16-, and 24-inch lengths. Cut the straw lengthwise into halves (see diagram). Then cut the straw halves to one 4½- and two 1½-inch lengths.

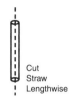

Cut Straw Lengthwise

what children do ✋

1. Cut out kite and bows from the pattern.
2. Print "Seek the Kingdom of God" on the front of the kite.
3. Glue the flattened 4½-inch straw from the top to the bottom on the back of the kite (see diagram).
4. Glue the 1½-inch straws on either side of the longer straw and flatten them.
5. On the front of the kite, tape the end of the 4-inch ribbon to the left and right corners.
6. Tape one end of the 16-inch ribbon to the top of the kite, then tape the ribbon about 7 inches down near the bottom of the kite, allowing the excess to hang for the tail.
7. Join the 4- and 16-inch ribbons together with the 24-inch ribbon, allowing the excess to hang for the kite's string.
8. Print "above" on the first bow, "all" on the second and "else" on the third. Evenly space and glue the bows on the tails.

4.5" Straw Half

1.5" Straw Half

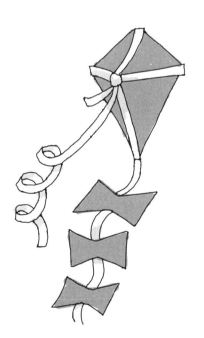

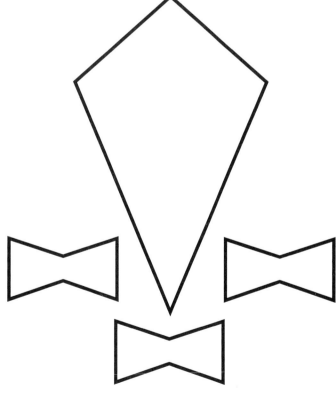

The Kingdom of God

Everything Is Possible with God (based on Mark 10:23–31)

memory verse 📖

Seek the Kingdom of God above all else.
Matthew 6:33

discussion questions 💬

1. What is the Kingdom of God?
2. What is something you can give up to follow Jesus?

Jesus Speaks to a Young Rich Man

Jesus Heals Ten Men

memory verse 📖

I will thank the LORD because he is just; I will sing praise to the name of the LORD Most High.
Psalm 7:17

One Man Thanks Jesus (based on Luke 17:11–19)

Jesus was traveling to Jerusalem one day when he met ten men outside of a village. These ten men lived outside the village gates because they had a disease called leprosy. Leprosy is a very contagious skin condition that they didn't have a cure for in Bible times.

When the ten men saw Jesus, they cried out, "Jesus, Master, have mercy on us!" They wanted Jesus to cure them of their leprosy.

Jesus looked at the ten men and said "Go show yourselves to the priests." As they walked away, all ten men were healed of their leprosy!

The men were amazed at their new skin. Nine of them continued to the priests, as Jesus had said. But one man turned around and went back to Jesus. Seeing Jesus again, the man fell to his knees and shouted, "Praise God!" He was so thankful for what Jesus had done.

Seeing that only one man had returned to thank him, Jesus said to the man, "Didn't I heal ten men? Where are the other nine? Has no one returned to give glory to God?"

Then, Jesus said to the one man who said thanks, "Stand up and go. Your faith has healed you."

Jesus has saved all of us from our sins. We can thank him in our worship and praise every day.

discussion questions 💬

1. What condition did the ten men have?
2. How can we thank Jesus?

One Thankful Hand

what you need ✑

- Scissors
- Crayons or markers

what you do ✂

Before class, photocopy this page, making one for each child.

what children do 🖐

1. Cut out the hand.
2. Draw polka dots on one side to represent the thankful man's leprosy.
3. On the other side, write, "Thank you, Jesus!" to show your thankfulness for Jesus. Decorate as you like.

what to say 📢

When Jesus healed the man who had leprosy, he was so thankful that he couldn't help but praise Jesus! Decorate this hand to remind yourself to thank Jesus often.

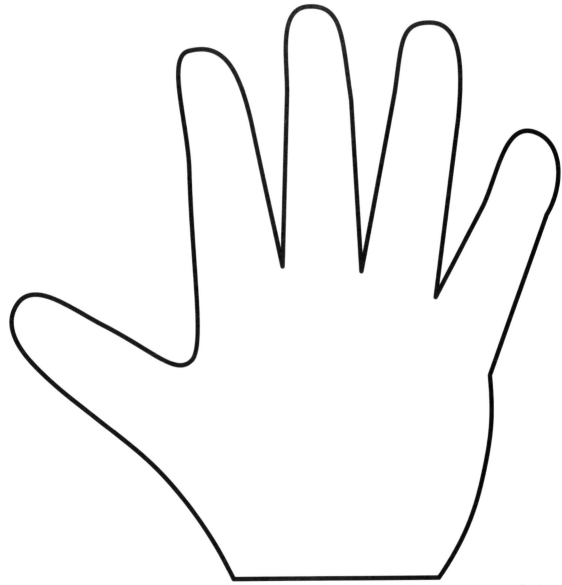

Spread the News

what you need ✎

- Scissors
- Glue
- Styrofoam cups, two for each child
- Pencil
- Yarn

what you do ✂

Before class, photocopy this page, making one for each child. Make a sample to demonstrate.

what children do 🖐

1. Cut out memory verse boxes.
2. Glue memory verse boxes to two separate Styrofoam cups.
3. Poke hole in bottom of each cup with a pencil.
4. Thread yarn through holes and tie to connect the cups.
5. Pair up and say the first part of the memory verse into the cup while a partner listens.
   Then switch as the partner recites the second half of the verse.

I will thank the LORD because he is just;

I will sing praise to the name of the LORD Most High.

Psalm 7:17

Thank You Chain

what you need

- Colored paper
- Scissors
- Tape

what you do ✂

Before class, photocopy this page on colored paper, making one for each child.

what children do ✋

1. Cut out each link.
2. Tape the end of your chain links together, linking each new one into the one just taped. Make sure the words face outward.
3. Now that you have a chain. Tear off a link each day this week and thank God for what is printed on it.

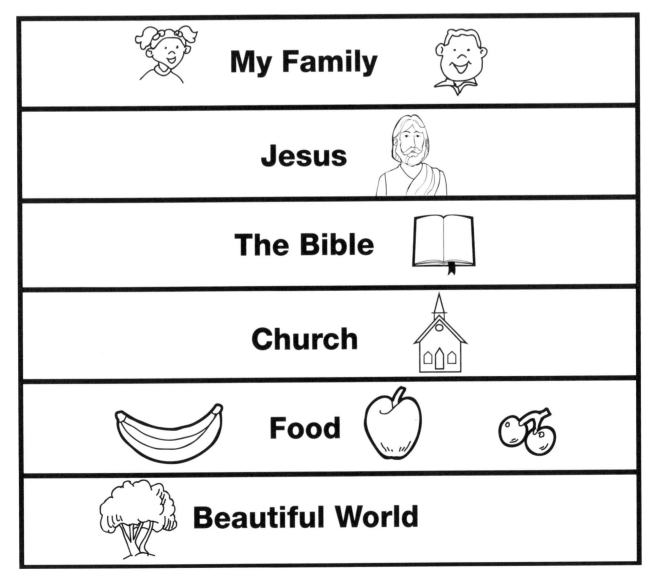

Jesus Heals Ten Men

One Man Thanks Jesus (based on Mark 10:23–31)

memory verse 📖

I will thank the LORD because he is just; I will sing praise to the name of the LORD Most High.
Psalm 7:17

discussion questions 💬

1. What condition did the ten men have?
2. How can we thank Jesus?

Responding to God's Love

Write the first letter of each object in the wheel below, starting with the top, and going clockwise to fill in the blank.

Give _____ to the Lord!

Jesus Raises Lazarus

memory verse 📖

God is our merciful Father and the source of all comfort.
2 Corinthians 1:3

From Sad to Glad (based on John 11:1–45)

A man named Lazarus had two sisters named Mary and Martha. Lazarus, Mary, and Martha were three of Jesus' good friends. Lazarus became very sick, so Mary and Martha sent a message to let Jesus know.

When Jesus received the message about his friend's illness, he remained calm. Even though Mary and Martha were sure Lazarus would die, Jesus said, "Lazarus's sickness will not end in death." Instead of rushing to Lazarus's bedside, Jesus remained where he was for two days.

Lazarus had been dead for four days when Jesus arrived. Martha said to Jesus, "Lord, if only you had been here, my brother would not have died." Jesus saw how sad Mary and Martha were, and he cried with them.

When Jesus, Mary, and Martha arrived at Lazarus's tomb, Jesus said, "Roll the stone aside." Many people had gathered to see what would happen.

Mary and Martha were surprised. "Lord," Martha said, "he has been dead for four days. The smell will be terrible."

But Jesus insisted, so they rolled the stone away from the front of the tomb. Jesus prayed. Then, he shouted, "Lazarus, come out!"

Everyone was amazed when they saw Lazarus walk out of the grave! He was covered in the cloth that Mary and Martha had buried him in. Jesus brought Lazarus back to life! Mary and Martha were so happy, and others around them believed in Jesus because of what he had done.

discussion questions 💬

1. Why did Jesus cry?
2. Has Jesus ever helped you when you were sad?

Clothespin Storytelling

what you need ✎

- Crayons or markers
- Scissors
- Glue
- Construction paper
- Tape
- Clothespins, three per child

what you do ✂

Before class, photocopy this page, making one for each child.

what children do ✋

1. Color and cut out the figures.
2. Glue figures to construction paper for stability and cut out again.
3. Tape a clothespin near the bottom of each figure to make a stand.
4. Move the figures around to retell the story of Jesus, Mary, Martha, and Lazarus.

Jesus' Message

what you need ✎

- Crayons or markers

what you do ✂

Before class, photocopy this page, making one for each child.

what children do ✋

1. Crack the code to see what Jesus said to Martha.

what to say 📣

Martha met Jesus outside her home as he arrived after Lazarus' death. She told him that she wished he had come before, but she knew even though Lazarus had died that Jesus could use his power to help. Since Jesus raised Lazarus from the dead, we know that he has power over death. Jesus is God's Son. He died on the cross so that we could have eternal life. We just have to believe in him.

A	B	C		J	K	L		S	T	U
D	E	F		M	N	O		V	W	X
G	H	I		P	Q	R		Y	Z	

J E _ _ _ _ _ _ _ _ _ _ _ _ _

_ _ _ _ _ _ _ _ _ _

_ _ _ _ , _ _ _ _ _ _ _ _

_ _ _ _ _ _ _ _ _ _ _ _ _ _

_ _ _ _ _ _ _ _ _ _ _ _

_ _ _ _ _ 11:25

Thankful for Jesus

what you need

- Scissors
- Crayons or markers

what you do ✂

Before class, photocopy this page, making one for each child.

what children do ✋

1. Cut out the heart.
2. Use the heart to draw a picture or write a story or song—or both!

what to say 📢

Mary, Martha, and Lazarus loved Jesus with all their heart. They were so thankful when Jesus raised Lazarus from the dead! Use this heart to show your love and thankfulness for Jesus drawing a picture or writing a story or song.

Jesus Raises Lazarus

From Sad to Glad (based on John 11:1–45)

memory verse 📖

God is our merciful Father and the source of all comfort.

2 Corinthians 1:3

discussion questions 💬

1. Why did Jesus cry?
2. Has Jesus ever helped you when you were sad?

Back to Life

Make a folding scene to remember that Jesus conquers death. Fold along the dotted lines and write the memory verse on the inside.

Jesus Blesses Children

memory verse

Jesus said, "Let the children come to me."
Matthew 19:14

Jesus Loves Children (based on Mark 10:13–16)

When Jesus lived on Earth, he performed many miracles and taught many wonderful things. People came from all around to hear him speak and to receive healing or his blessing. Once, when Jesus was teaching, some parents brought their children to Jesus so he could bless them.

Many religious leaders and teachers during this time thought they were too busy to talk to children. They didn't want anything to do with them! When the parents brought their children to Jesus, the disciples thought Jesus would be too busy, too.

"Keep your children away!" They said. "Don't you know how important this man is?"

When Jesus saw this happen, he was angry with his disciples. "Let the children come to me," he said. "Don't stop them! For the Kingdom of God belongs to those who are like these children."

Then, Jesus took the children in his arms and blessed them.

Jesus showed kindness to the children because he loves them. In fact, Jesus loves everyone!

discussion questions

1. Why did the disciples try to keep the children away?
2. How can you show Jesus' love and kindness to others?

Solve the Puzzle

what you need

- Crayons or markers
- Scissors
- Glue
- Construction paper

what you do ✂

Before class, photocopy this page, making one for each child.

what children do ✋

1. Color and cut out the solid border of the picture.
2. Glue picture to construction paper.
3. Carefully cut on the dashed lines.
4. Turn the puzzle pieces face down and mix them up. Try to fit the puzzle together correctly without flipping over the pieces. When you think you've got it, flip it over to see how you did.

Jesus Loves Me Reminder

what you need

- Paper plates
- Scissors
- Paper
- Crayons or markers
- Stapler
- Glue
- Hole punch
- Ribbon

what you do ✂

Before class, photocopy this page, making one for each child. Cut some paper plates in half so each child has one whole plate and one half plate. Cut paper into small strips for children to write on, several strips per child.

what children do ✋

1. Line up and staple the half plate to the whole plate, stapling along the rounded edge but leaving the cut side open.
2. Color and cut out the acorns and "Jesus Loves Me" sign.
3. Glue acorns and sign to the plate and decorate as you like.
4. Punch two holes at the top of the plate.
5. Thread and knot a piece of ribbon to make a hanger.
6. Write or draw on the slips things that remind you of Jesus' love (home, church, pets, family, friends, etc.) and place the slips in the holder.

Finished Reminder

Jesus Loves Me

Children Come to Jesus Maze

what you need ✏️

• Crayons or markers

what you do ✂️

Before class, photocopy this page, making one for each child.

what children do ✋

1. Trace your way through the maze to help the children visit Jesus.

what to say 📢

Jesus was kind to the children because he loves everyone. Can you help these children make their way through the maze to find Jesus?

Jesus Blesses Children

Jesus Loves Children (based on John 11:1–45)

memory verse 📖

Jesus said, "Let the children come to me."
Matthew 19:14

discussion questions 💬

1. Why did the disciples try to keep the children away?
2. How can you show Jesus' love and kindness to others?

Showing Kindness Book

Jesus was kind to children because he loves them. Which of the children below are following Jesus' example by being kind?

1. Color and cut out the pictures of the kind kids. Mark an X over the pictures of the foolish kids.
2. In the empty box, draw a picture of you being kind to someone else.
3. Color and cut the box with the memory verse.
4. Place the cut out squares into a stack with the memory verse on top.
5. Staple the squares together on the left side at the top and bottom to make a book.

A Lost Sheep

memory verse 📖

[God said,] I myself will search and find my sheep.
Ezekiel 34:11

Searching for One Lost Sheep (based on Luke 15:1–7)

All sorts of people came to speak to Jesus. Even sinners and people who weren't popular wanted to hear what Jesus had to say. No matter who came, Jesus welcomed anyone who would listen. Sometimes, he even shared meals with them.

This upset some religious leaders and teachers. They thought that someone who claimed to be God's Son shouldn't be around such sinful people, let alone eat with them!

When people started to complain, Jesus told a story.

"If a man has a hundred sheep and one of them gets lost, what will he do? Won't he leave the ninety-nine others in the wilderness and go to search for the one that is lost until he finds it?"

The people nodded their head yes.

"And when he finds it," Jesus continued, "The shepherd would be so excited. He would celebrate and tell everyone he knows that he found his lost sheep."

"Heaven is like that," Jesus said. "There is more joy in Heaven over one lost sinner who repents and returns to God than over ninety-nine others who are righteous and haven't strayed away!"

Jesus taught that he came to Earth to save everyone. No matter how we've sinned, Jesus died for us! He accepts us and makes us new.

discussion questions 💬

1. Why were some people upset with Jesus?
2. How do you feel when you find something you've lost?

Lost or Found?

what you need ✏

- Crayons or markers

what you do ✂

Before class, photocopy this page, making one for each child.

what children do ✋

1. Read each sentence below.
2. If you think a statement will make God sad, write L for LOST inside the sheep. If you think the statement will please God, write F for FOUND inside the sheep.

 1. I will not be friends with you anymore.

 2. You can take a turn ahead of me.

 3. Thank you for taking care of me, Mother.

 4. I don't want to go to church.

 5. May I help carry your groceries?

 6. How can you be so stupid?

 7. You're the best Grandpa in the world!

 8. I'm sorry if I hurt your feelings.

 9. I'll do my chores when I feel like it.

 10. Listen to the Bible verse I just learned!

 11. I can't stand you.

 12. I'll pray for you this week.

Sheepfold

what you need 🖌

- Scissors
- Black markers
- Ruler
- Green and brown paper, one of both colors for each child
- Glue

what you do ✂

Before class, photocopy this page, making one for each child.

what children do ✋

1. Cut out the sheep.
2. On the first sheep write "God said." On the second write "I myself will search." On the third write "and find my sheep."
3. Cut squares of brown construction paper that are approximately 1-inch in size.
4. Glue the brown squares around the edges of the green paper. This is the wall of your sheepfold.
5. Glue the sheep in the sheepfold.

what to say 📢

Jesus is your faithful shepherd. You are like his sheep. If you disobey God and wander away from his rules, he will look for you. When he finds you, he will bring you back joyfully.

Moveable Sheep

what you need ✏

- Glue
- Poster board
- Scissors
- Cotton balls
- Hole punch
- Paper fasteners

what you do ✂

Before class, photocopy this page, making one for each child.

what children do ✋

1. Glue the sheep on the poster board and then cut it out.
2. Glue little pieces of cotton on the sheep picture.
3. Place the legs on the sheep and punch a hole through both at the small crosses.
4. Connect the legs to the sheep with paper fasteners.
5. Move the sheep's legs so it will lie down to sleep or make the sheep stand up to eat.
6. Pretend you are the Good Shepherd and find a place for your sheep to sleep and eat.

A Lost Sheep

Searching for One Lost Sheep (based on Luke 15:1–7)

memory verse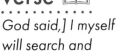

God said,] I myself will search and find my sheep.
Ezekiel 34:11

discussion questions

1. Why were some people upset with Jesus?
2. How do you feel when you find something you've lost?

Bring Back the Sheep

Complete the verse to help the sheep find their way home. Follow the line from each sheep to its blank and fill in the blank with the word on the sheep.

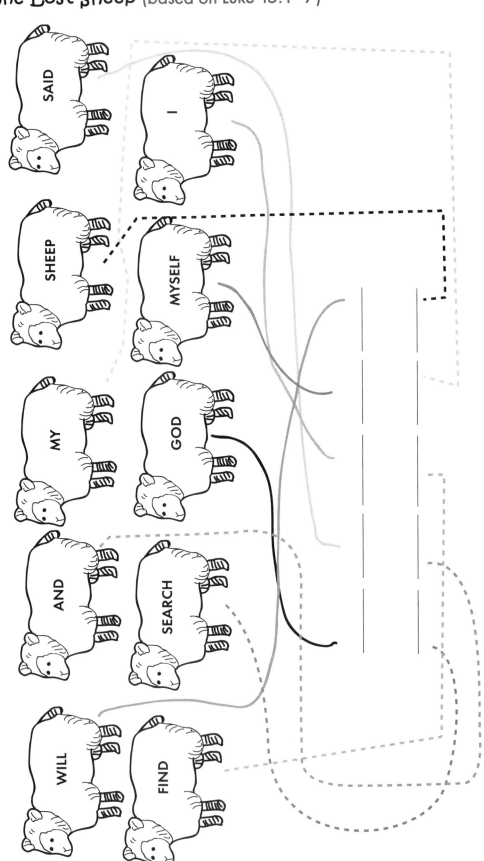

SAID

—

SHEEP

MYSELF

MY

GOD

AND

SEARCH

WILL

FIND

chapter 36

A Woman's Lost Coin

memory verse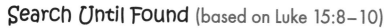

[Jesus] came to seek and save those who are lost.
Luke 19:10

Search Until Found (based on Luke 15:8–10)

Jesus was different from other teachers during his day. He welcomed everyone who listened to him. He wanted everyone to hear the Good News he had to share.

Sometimes, people who weren't very popular listened to Jesus. Other religious people didn't like this. They thought these people were too sinful to hear what Jesus had to say. They complained that Jesus couldn't really be God's Son if he spoke to these sinful people.

When people started to complain, Jesus told a story.

"Imagine a woman has ten silver coins and she loses one," Jesus said. "What would she do? The woman would search her entire house for it! She would turn on all lights, sweep the floor, and look through all the furniture until she found the coin."

"When she finds the coin," Jesus continued, "She will be so excited. She'll tell all her friends and neighbors the good news."

"Heaven is like that," Jesus said. "Heaven rejoices when even one sinner repents."

We're all sinners. That's why Jesus came to Earth to save everyone. Jesus showed love to everyone around him, and we can too.

discussion questions

1. What did the woman in the story do to find her lost coin?
2. How is Heaven like this story?

181

Story Order Race

what you need

- Crayons or markers
- Scissors

what you do ✂

Before class, photocopy this page, making one for each child. When children finish coloring and cutting out the pictures, say "Go" to begin the race. The first to finish answers a discussion question.

what children do ✋

1. Color the pictures and cut them apart.
2. Turn the pictures over and mix them up.
3. When your teacher says "Go," race to be the first to arrange the pictures in story order.

what to say 📢

When the woman in the story lost her coin, she rushed to find it. Can you rush to arrange these pictures in story order?

Seek and Save Magnifying Glass

what you need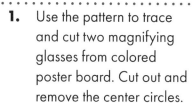

- Plastic transparency sheets or clear Con-Tact paper
- Scissors
- Colored poster board
- Glue
- Crayons or markers

what you do ✂

Before class, photocopy this page, making one for each child. Cut the transparency sheets or clear Con-Tact paper into squares large enough to cover the opening, one for each child. If using clear Con-Tact paper, cut two sheets that children can place on either side of the magnifying glass, stick sides together.

what children do ✋

1. Use the pattern to trace and cut two magnifying glasses from colored poster board. Cut out and remove the center circles.
2. Apply glue to the outer ring of one magnifying glass and set a plastic sheet over the hole.
3. Apply glue to the outer edges of the other ring and place it on the first one. If the plastic sheet edges show, trim them off.
4. Write the memory verse on the handle.

what to say 📢

The woman in the story looked everywhere for her lost coin, just like Jesus seeks and saves us. Make this magnifying glass so you remember that Jesus searches for us.

Lost Coin Search

what you need ✎

- Crayons or markers

what you do ✂

Before class, photocopy this page, making one for each child.

what children do ✋

1. Color the picture.
2. Draw a circle around all of the silly things in the picture.
3. Help the woman searching for her lost money by circling the coins.

One pant leg is shorter than the other, raccoon on the floor, elephant table legs, clown in picture, snowman looking in the window.

A Woman's Lost Coin

Search Until Found (based on Luke 15:1–7)

memory verse 📖

[Jesus] came to seek and save those who are lost.
Luke 19:10

discussion questions 💬

1. Why were some people upset with Jesus?
2. How do you feel when you find something you've lost?

Party Piñata

The woman who found the lost coin gave a wonderful party for her friends and neighbors. She was excited and happy to have found her lost coin. She had searched and searched throughout her house just to find it. Make a Party Piñata to show how happy she was.

1. Open paper lunch sack.

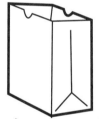

2. Cut tissue paper into two 3x18-inch strips. Snip to create fringe.

3. Glue one tissue paper strip around bottom of bag and one 3" above bottom.

4. Cut and glue tissue squares on bag.

5. Stuff bag with newspaper or tissue and treats.

6. Fold over top corners and staple.

7. Punch holes in top of bag.

8. Thread a ribbon hanger through holes.

finished piñata

The Prodigal Son

memory verse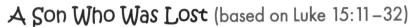

God is . . . forgiving.
Daniel 9:9

A Son Who Was Lost (based on Luke 15:11–32)

Jesus once told a story about two sons. Both sons had a father who was going to give them all his money when he died.

The older son stayed home with his father and helped take care of their house and farm. The younger son grew impatient. He told his father that he wanted his share of the money now, before the father died.

The father agreed to give the younger son his money, so he packed all his money and moved to a far away land. Away from home, the younger son did anything he wanted. But he quickly spent all his money. When his money ran out, a famine also came through the land, and he began to starve.

Eventually, a farmer hired the younger son to take care of some pigs. The younger son was so hungry that he ate the pigs' food!

Finally, the son came to his sense. "I had food and servants at home, but I'm dying of hunger here! I'm going back to my father." So the son returned to his father, hoping that his father would take him in as a servant.

The father spotted his son as he was on his way home. Seeing his son, the father ran to him, gave him a hug, and kissed him. The father asked his servants to bring his younger son new clothes and to prepare a party in his honor.

At first, the older son was jealous. He had been working for his father for so long, but his father never threw him a party.

The father responded, "We had to celebrate this happy day. For your brother was dead and has come back to life! He was lost, but now he is found!"

Jesus said Heaven is like this. God, our Heavenly Father, is so excited when we return to him!

discussion questions

1. How did the father respond to his younger son's return?
2. How is God like the father in the story?

Run Away Maze

what you need 🖌

• Crayons or markers

what you do ✂

Before class, photocopy this page, making one for each child.

what children do ✋

1. Find the prodigal son's path to the far away country in the center of the maze. Then, find his bath back to his father.

Start

Finish

Wise Words Stand-Up

what you need

- Crayons or markers
- Scissors
- Construction paper
- Glue

what you do

Before class, photocopy this page, making one for each child.

what children do

1. Color any space with a black dot red to reveal the wise words.
2. Color the other spaces in any color you want.
3. Cut out each picture.
4. Fold a piece of construction paper in half lengthwise to form a stand.
5. Glue one picture to each side to remember these wise words.

what to say

The son who left home told his father, "I'm sorry." The father's actions showed the boy that he was forgiven. God always forgives us when we do wrong. When we say, "I am sorry," God answers, "I forgive you." Saying "I'm sorry" to people you have wronged may help them forgive you, too.

Different Sons

what you need 🖌

- Crayons or markers

what you do ✂

Before class, photocopy this page, making one for each child.

what children do ✋

1. Look at each row of pictures. Which object is different from the others?
2. Circle the different object in each row.
3. Color the pictures.

what to say 📢

The two sons in the story acted very differently from one another. Even though they were different, the father loved both of his sons.

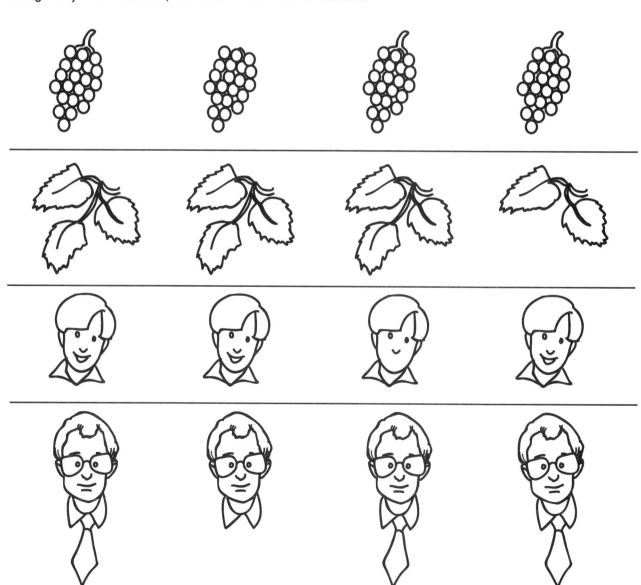

The Prodigal Son

A Son Who Was Lost (based on Luke 15:11–32)

memory verse

God is . . . forgiving.

Daniel 9:9

discussion questions

1. How did the father respond to his younger son's return?
2. How is God like the father in the story?

A Forgiving Father

God is our Heavenly Father. He loves you, and he wants you to come home. Use the code below to write something you need forgiveness for. Tell that to God. Then, draw a picture of you running to God, the Father.

Father   Me

_____

A	B	C	D	E	F	G	H	I	J	K	L	M	N	O	P	Q	R	S	T	U	V	W	X	Y	Z
1	2	3	4	5	6	7	8	9	10	11	12	13	14	15	16	17	18	19	20	21	22	23	24	25	26

Jesus Heals a Blind Man

memory verse 📖

Give thanks to the LORD, for he is good!
Psalm 106:1

Beautiful Sights (based on Luke 18:35–43)

One day, a blind man was sitting by the road, begging for money. He couldn't see what was happening, but suddenly the crowd around him started making a lot of noise.

"What's happening?" the blind man asked anyone who would hear him.

"It's Jesus!" Someone replied "He's walking this way down the road! I can't believe it's him!"

The blind man was amazed. *Maybe Jesus can help me*, he thought. The blind man started shouting to get Jesus' attention. "Jesus! Jesus! I'm over here!" The blind man shouted. "Help me, please, Jesus!"

People in the crowd told the man to be quiet, but he only started shouting louder.

When Jesus heard the man, he asked someone to bring him to him. When Jesus finally saw the man, he asked, "What do you want me to do for you?"

"Lord," the blind man said, "I want to see!"

"Your faith has healed you!" Jesus responded. Instantly, the man's eyes were opened, and he could see! The man couldn't believe it. That day, he began following Jesus, praising God everywhere he went.

discussion questions 🗩

1. Why was the blind man healed?
2. How can you have faith like the blind man?

Finish the Story

what you need ✎

- Crayons or markers

what you do ✂

Before class, photocopy this page, making one for each child.

what children do ✋

1. Below are words spelled backward. Write all the words correctly on the numbered blank lines below.

2. Complete the story by printing the number of the correct word in the blanks. Two words are used more than once.

1.	THGIS	**6.**	DNILB	**11.**	YPPAH
2.	EES	**7.**	HTIAF	**12.**	DEIRC
3.	DESIARP	**8.**	DAS	**13.**	RETSAM
4.	REHTO	**9.**	NWOT	**14.**	DEWOLLOF
5.	SUSEJ	**10.**	GNINEPPAH		

1. _____	**6.** _____	**11.** _____
2. _____	**7.** _____	**12.** _____
3. _____	**8.** _____	**13.** _____
4. _____	**9.** _____	**14.** _____
5. _____	**10.** _____	

A _____ man sat by the road. He was _____. Jesus went by on his way to _____. A large crowd came with him. The blind man could hear the noise. "What is _____?" he asked.

"_____ is coming," they said.

The blind man was _____. He called, "_____, help me!"

"Shh," hushed the people who led the crowd. "Don't bother Jesus." The blind man _____ even louder.

Jesus asked for the blind man to be brought to him. Jesus asked how he could help.

"Please, _____. Help me _____," the blind man asked.

"Receive your _____," Jesus said. "Your _____ has healed you."

In a moment's time, the man could see. He _____ Jesus. He didn't have to beg anymore. He _____ God. He was so _____. And when _____ people saw, they _____ God, too!

Meeting Jesus

what you need ✎

- Crayons or markers
- Scissors
- Stapler
- Pencils, one for each child

what you do ✂

Before class, photocopy this page, making one for each child.

what children do ✋

1. Color both kneeling men exactly the same. Color Jesus.
2. Cut out Figure A on the dashed lines.
3. Staple Figure A over Figure B on the solid line.
4. Wrap the top picture tightly around a pencil, from left to right, two or three times.
5. Now, roll the pencil from right to left quickly, unwrapping the top picture completely.
6. Repeat again and again to watch the blind man see.

what to say 📢

The blind man's love for Jesus resulted in others also believing in him. Make a moving picture of the blind man receiving his sight and reaching out to Jesus.

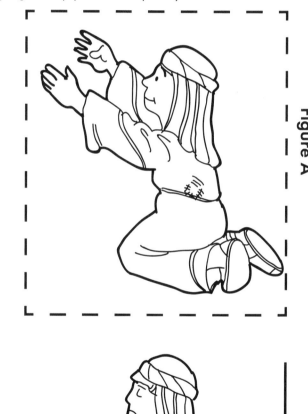

Figure A

Figure B

Faith of a Blind Man

what you need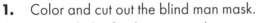

- Crayons or markers
- Scissors
- Hole punch
- Craft sticks
- Glue

what you do ✂

Before class, photocopy this page, making one for each child.

what children do ✋

1. Color and cut out the blind man mask.
2. Cut out holes for the eyes and mouth. Use a hole punch to get started.
3. Glue a craft stick to the bottom of the back side of the mask.
4. Hold the mask up to your face to act out the story.

 Top 50 Bible Stories about Jesus for Elementary.

Jesus Heals a Blind Man

Beautiful Sights (based on Luke 18:35–43)

memory verse 📖

Give thanks to the LORD, for he is good!
Psalm 106:1

discussion questions 💬

1. Why was the blind man healed?
2. How can you have faith like the blind man?

A-maze-ing Faith

The blind man had faith that Jesus could heal him. He couldn't stop praising Jesus once when he could see again.

Trace through the maze to help Jesus find his way to heal the blind man.

Start

Finish

Jesus & Zacchaeus

memory verse 📖

You are my friends if you do what I command.
John 15:14

A Lonely Little Man (based on Luke 19:1–10)

A man named Zacchaeus wanted to see Jesus when he was visiting his town. Zacchaeus was the chief tax collector in his region, and he was very rich. People didn't like tax collectors in Bible times, so Zacchaeus didn't have many friends.

Huge crowds gathered almost anywhere Jesus went. Everyone wanted to see him! When Jesus was in Zacchaeus's town, the crowds were too big for Zacchaeus to see!

Zacchaeus knew exactly what to do. He ran ahead of the crowd and climbed into a big tree beside the road so he could see over the crowd.

His plan worked! He could see Jesus walking by. Zacchaeus was so excited to see Jesus. Then, something surprising happened.

Seeing Zacchaeus in the tree, Jesus stopped and said, "Zacchaeus! Come down from the tree! Let me be a guest in your house today."

Zacchaeus couldn't believe what he heard. He climbed down from the tree and took Jesus to his house.

Some people didn't like that Jesus was visiting a tax collector. But Jesus wanted to show that he loves everyone.

Zacchaeus told Jesus that he would give half of his wealth to the poor and that he would return money to people he cheated on their taxes.

Jesus was very pleased. "Salvation has come to this home today," he said. That day, Zacchaeus was saved for his faith in Jesus.

discussion questions 💬

1. Why did people dislike Zacchaeus?
2. How did Zacchaeus show faith?

Zacchaeus's Tree

what you need 🖌

- Scissors
- Yarn
- Ruler

- Tape
- Crayons or markers
- Hole punch

- Cotton balls
- Glue

what you do ✂

Before class, photocopy this page, making one for each child.

Cut yarn into 24-inch lengths, one for each child.

what children do ✋

1. Tightly wrap tape around one end of the yarn to make it like the end of a shoestring.
2. Color and cut out one Zacchaeus and two tree patterns.
3. Glue Zacchaeus in the tree on one side.
4. Write the memory verse on the other side of the tree. Place one tree pattern on top of the other and punch holes where indicated.
5. Lace the circles together with the yarn, leave an opening at the bottom of the tree trunk.
6. Stuff the tree with cotton balls.
7. Finish lacing and tie the ends in a bow. Trim the ends.

Up in a Tree

what you need ✏

- Crayons or markers

what you do ✂

Before class, photocopy this page, making one for each child.

what children do ✋

1. Help Zacchaeus climb the tree. Follow the maze from Zacchaeus at the bottom to the branch at the top so he can see Jesus.

Climbing Man

what you need ✏

- Scissors
- Construction paper
- Crayons or markers
- Glue

what you do ✂

Before class, photocopy this page, making one for each child. Cut 5" x ½" wide strips from construction paper for arms and legs, four for each child.

what children do ✋

1. Cut out the pattern.
2. Cut four 5" x ½" wide strips from construction paper for arms and legs.
3. Draw a face on the man.
4. Accordion-fold the construction paper strips for arms and legs.
5. Glue the arms and legs in place.
6. Write the memory verse on the back.

finished craft

Jesus & Zacchaeus

A Lonely Little Man (based on Luke 19:1–10)

memory verse 📖

You are my friends if you do what I command.
John 15:14

discussion questions 💬

1. Why did people dislike Zacchaeus?
2. How did Zacchaeus show faith?

Finger Puppet Story

1. Color the finger puppets of Jesus and Zacchaeus and cut them out.
2. Curl the tabs backward and tape the ends of the tabs together so they will fit on your fingers.
3. Use the finger puppets to act out the story of Zacchaeus.

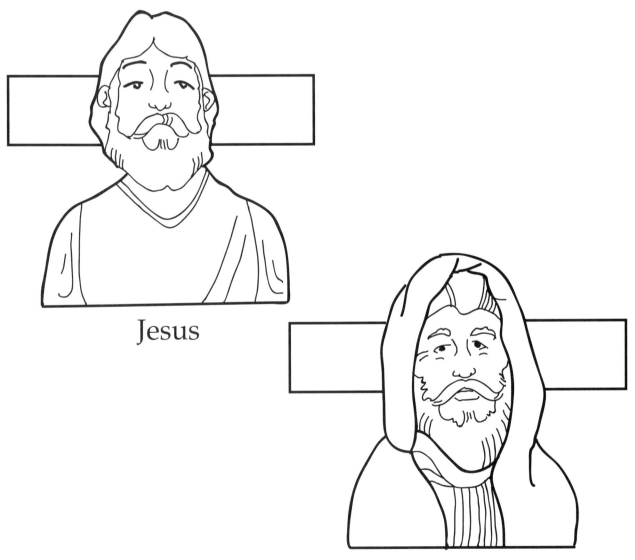

Jesus

Zacchaeus

Jesus Is the Good Shepherd

memory verse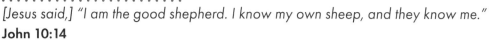

[Jesus said,] "I am the good shepherd. I know my own sheep, and they know me."
John 10:14

A Shepherd Gives His Life for His Sheep (based on John 10:1–18)

Jesus often used different illustrations or stories to explain the Bible to others. One of his stories were about sheep and shepherds.

"Anyone who sneaks over the wall of a sheepfold, rather than going through the gate, must surely be a thief and a robber!" Jesus said. "But the one who enters through the gate is the shepherd of the sheep."

Jesus explains that the gatekeeper and the sheep would recognize the true shepherd when he came. The sheep recognize the shepherd's voice, and they follow him.

At first, those listening to Jesus' story were confused. *Why was Jesus talking about sheep?* They wondered. So Jesus continued.

"I am the gate for the sheep," Jesus said. "Those who come in through me will be saved."

"I am the good shepherd," Jesus said. "I know my own sheep, and they know me, just as my Father knows me and I know the Father. So I sacrifice my life for the sheep."

Jesus told those who were listening that he had other sheep who were not yet in the sheepfold. He said it was his job to bring them.

Jesus was telling us that he came to save all of us. He came to find those of us who are lost. Jesus died for all of our sins.

discussion questions

1. How is Jesus like a shepherd?
2. How are you like a sheep?

Sheep and Shepherd Quiz

what you need

- Bibles
- Crayons or markers
- Glue
- Cotton balls

what you do ✂

Before class, photocopy this page, making one for each child.

what children do ✋

1. Read the statements in this quiz.
2. If the statement is true, glue a cotton ball on the sheep. If the statement is false, write an *F* inside that sheep.
3. Use a Bible to double-check your answers.

1. Shepherds enter sheepfolds through a hole in the top of the sheepfold.

2. There were no sheep thieves in Jesus' day.

3. Sheep will follow anyone carrying a shepherd's staff.

4. Shepherds walk in front of sheep to lead them.

5. Jesus said that he was the window for the sheep.

6. Jesus came to make life boring for everyone.

7. Helpers hired to care for sheep chased wolves with flutes.

8. Hired helpers loved the sheep less than the shepherds did.

9. Jesus said that he knows his sheep and his sheep know him.

10. A good shepherd runs and hides if he gets scared.

11. Jesus wanted other sheep invited into his fold.

12. Jesus said the people who came before him were aliens.

13. Jesus told this story to let us know that he died for us.

14. The Good Shepherd in this story was the ruler of Rome.

Sheep in the Fold

what you need

- Ruler
- Brown paper
- Scissors
- Crayons or markers
- Stapler
- White paper
- Glue

Finished Sheepfold

what you do ✂

Before class, photocopy this page, making one for each child. Cut paper into 8½-inch squares, one for each child.

what children do ✋

1. Color and cut out the picture.
2. Fold up the bottom of the picture and staple it to form a pocket as shown.
3. Trace sheep on white paper and cut them out.
4. Cut the brown paper in half to make doors.
5. Glue the doors over the dashed lines and fold them back to open them.
6. Tie closed the doors.

Glue door here

Glue door here

Fold up

Mystery Code Bible Verse

what you need ✎

- Crayons or markers

what you do ✂

Before class, photocopy this page, making one for each child.

what children do ✋

1. Break this code by counting two letters forward in the alphabet. What do you do about Y and Z? They become A and B, of course!
2. Write each letter on the blanks below.

Code Key

Code:	Y	Z	A	B	C	D	E	F	G	H	I	J	K	L	M	N	O	P	Q	R	S	T	U	V	W	X
Letter:	A	B	C	D	E	F	G	H	I	J	K	L	M	N	O	P	Q	R	S	T	U	V	W	X	Y	Z

G   Y   K   R   F   C   E   M   M   B   Q   F   C   N   F   C   P   B

___   ___   ___   ___   ___   ___   ___   ___   ___   ___   ___   ___   ___   ___   ___   ___   ___   ___

H   M   F   L

___ ___ ___ ___ 10:14

Jesus Is the Good Shepherd

A Shepherd Gives His Life for His Sheep (based on John 10:1–18)

memory verse 📖

[Jesus said,] "I am the good shepherd. I know my own sheep, and they know me."
John 10:14

discussion questions 💬

1. How is Jesus like a shepherd?
2. How are you like a sheep?

Good Shepherd

1. Color and cut out the shepherd and other items.
2. Glue the shepherd to construction paper.
3. Glue on his clothes, hat, and staff to prepare him for a day in the field.
4. Draw sheep in the background.

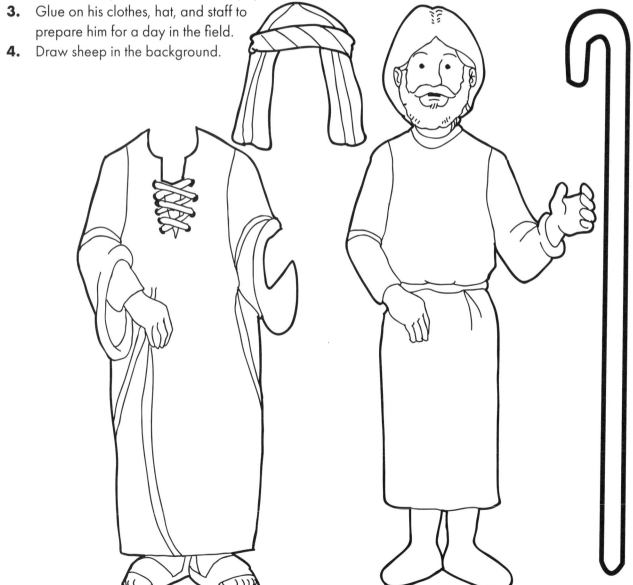

Section 3

Jesus' Last Days, Death, & Resurrection

The People Praise Jesus

memory verse 📖

How good to sing praises to our God!
Psalm 147:1

Jesus Enters Jerusalem (based on Matthew 21:1–11)

It was finally time for Jesus to enter Jerusalem. The prophets had said long ago that their new King would enter the city of Jerusalem to save his people, and that day had finally come.

Just outside the city, Jesus told some of his disciples to go to a nearby village. There, they would see a donkey and its colt. He wanted them to bring the donkey and its colt to him.

Jesus' disciples did as they were asked, and Jesus rode the donkey into Jerusalem.

Many people expected their King to come in on a beautiful horse. They were surprised to see Jesus ride in on a humble donkey!

When the crowd saw Jesus coming on the donkey, they began praising his name. Many of them spread their garments on the road ahead of him or spread palm branches for the donkey to walk on.

The people shouted, "Hosanna! Praise God in highest heaven! Jesus is here!"

discussion questions 💬

1. Why did Jesus ride a donkey into Jerusalem?
2. What did the people do when they saw Jesus?

Praise Jesus Windsock

what you need

- Bright crepe or tissue paper
- Scissors
- Empty, round oatmeal container
- Bright paper
- Glue
- Crayons and markers
- Tape
- Hole Punch
- Yarn

what you do ✂

Before class, photocopy this page, enlarging it by 200% and making one for each child.
Cut 1½x16-inch strips of bright crepe or tissue paper in two contrasting colors.

what children do ✋

1. Cover the outside of an empty oatmeal container with bright paper.
2. Cut out and glue a scalloped border on the top and bottom.
3. Color, cut out, and glue on the "Praise Jesus" box.
4. Tape one end of each crepe or tissue paper strip inside the lower rim of the box, alternating colors.
5. Punch three holes in the top.
6. Thread and tie yarn to hang.

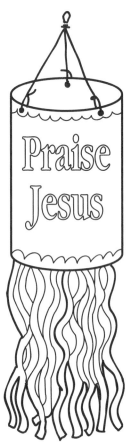

Pencil Praises

what you need ✏️

- Crayons or markers
- Scissors
- Hole punch
- Pencils, three for each child

what you do ✂️

Before class, photocopy this page, making one for each child.

what children do ✋

1. Color and cut out the pictures.
2. Punch a hole at the top and bottom of each picture.
3. Slip the pencils through the holes.
4. Keep the Pencil Praises or give them to a friend.

finished craft

Hosanna!

Praise Jesus!

Glory to God!

Musical Praise Code

what you need 🖌

- Crayons or markers

what you do ✂

Before class, photocopy this page, making one for each child.

what children do ✋

1. Use the musical code to find out six of the ways people in the Bible praised Jesus.

what to say 📢

There are many different ways we can praise God. Can you think of
ways we can use each of those words to praise God today?

Exodus 15:1

Psalm 145:10–11

Psalm 47:1

Psalm 32:11

Psalm 95:6

Psalm 75:1

The People Praise Jesus

Jesus Enters Jerusalem (based on Matthew 21:1–11)

memory verse

How good to sing praises to our God!
Psalm 147:1

Finished Headband

discussion questions

1. Why did Jesus ride a donkey into Jerusalem?
2. What did the people do when they saw Jesus?

Praise Jesus Headband

1. Cut out the patterns (the headband needs to be cut and traced on a sheet of folded paper).
2. Fold a piece of a paper in half and place the headband pattern on the fold.
3. Trace the headband pattern onto the folded paper and cut it out.
4. Unfold the headband and glue the letters in place.
5. Punch holes on the sides, as shown.
6. String 24-inch lengths of narrow ribbon on the sides of the headband for ties.
7. Knot the ribbons, as shown, to hold the ties in place.

✄ **Place on fold.**

Jesus & the Poor Widow

memory verse 📖

[Share] all good things.
Galatians 6:6

Everything She Had (based on Mark 12:41–44; Luke 21:1–4)

When Jesus was in Jerusalem, he visited the Temple. Entering the Temple, Jesus sat beside the collection box, where people gave their offerings to the Temple.

Jesus saw many people give money that day. Rich and wealthy came by, dropping large amounts into the box. It was easy for them to give.

Then, a poor widow came by herself. She wore humble clothes and held a small moneybag. Passing by the collection box, the poor widow dropped in two small coins. It was all she had.

Seeing what she had done, Jesus called to his disciples. "This poor widow has given more than all the others," he said. "For they gave a tiny part of their money, but she, poor as she is, has given everything she had to live on."

Giving isn't about how much we can give. God isn't always impressed by huge amounts of money! Instead, God cares about how and why we give.

discussion questions 💬

1. What was the difference between how the rich people gave and how the poor widow gave?
2. What do you have to give to God?

Pretty Penny Coin Bag

what you need ✏

- Craft foam, felt, lightweight poster board, or construction paper
- Yarn
- Ruler
- Scissors
- Hole punch
- Markers

what you do ✂

Before class, photocopy this page, making one for each child. Cut one 48-inch length of yarn for each child.

what children do ✋

1. Use the pattern to trace and cut one purse from craft foam, felt, lightweight poster board, or construction paper.
2. Cut a slit on the lower flap.
3. Punch holes along the sides as indicated.
4. Take the length of yarn and fold it in half.
5. Fold the flap up and line up the holes. Begin lacing the purse from the bottom right.
6. Continue upward, leaving a length of yarn about 9 inches long across the top for a handle before starting down the opposite side. Tie off the ends.
7. Insert the top tab into the slit.
8. Write the memory verse on the back of the coin bag.

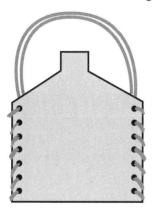

Giving Generously

what you need ✐

- Crayons or markers

what you do ✂

Before class, photocopy this page, making one for each child.

what children do ✋

1. In each situation, circle the children who are giving generously.
2. Draw your own situation and choices in the blank boxes.

Sharing Poster

what you need

- Crayons
- Pennies, two per child
- Scissors

what you do ✂

Before class, photocopy this page, making one for each child. Be sure to enlarge the rectangle as you photocopy it, making it as large as you can. Give each child two pennies.

what children do ✋

1. Cut out the blank poster below.
2. Place the pennies under this paper, centered on the poster area.
3. Rub over the pennies with the flat side of a crayon to make a crayon etching.
4. Write the memory verse at the bottom of the poster.
5. Give your pennies during your church's offering. Decorate the rest of the poster with other things you can give.

Jesus & the Poor Widow

Everything She Had (based on Mark 12:41–44; Luke 21:1–4)

memory verse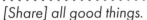

[Share] all good things.
Galatians 6:6

discussion questions 💬

1. What was the difference between how the rich people gave and how the poor widow gave?
2. What do you have to give to God?

Share-It Popper

The woman in the story shared what she had. You can create this popper to share with a friend or family member.

1. Color and cut out the wrapper.
2. Cut a toilet-paper tube in half.
3. Stuff each half with treats.
4. Holding the two halves together, wrap the tube with tissue paper.
5. Tie the ends with ribbon.
6. Glue the wrapper on one side of the popper. Decorate as you like.
7. Share the popper with a friend or family member.

Share

[Share] all good things.
Galatians 6:6

Share

Jesus Washes the Disciples' Feet

memory verse 📖

Serve one another in love.
Galatians 5:13

An Example to Follow (based on John 13:1–17)

It was time to celebrate the feast of Passover. Jesus and all his disciples gathered and prepared a meal to celebrate. Everyone was seated at the table and ready to eat.

Before the meal began, though, Jesus got up from the table and took off his outer robe, and tied a towel around his waist. He was dressed as a servant! Then, Jesus poured water into a basin. "Let me wash your feet," he told his disciples.

In Bible times, people wore sandals on dusty, dirty roads. Usually, humble servants washed rich people's feet. It was a pretty gross job. The disciples were amazed that Jesus wanted to do this.

Peter, one of Jesus' disciples, couldn't believe it. "You will never wash my feet!" Peter said.

Jesus told Peter, "Unless I wash you, you won't belong to me."

Finally, Peter agreed. Jesus washed Peter's feet and all the other disciples' feet, too. When he was finished, Jesus returned to the table.

"Since I, your Lord and Teacher, have washed your feet, you ought to wash each other's feet," Jesus said. "I have given you an example to follow. Do as I have done to you."

discussion questions 💬

1. Why did Jesus wash his disciples' feet?
2. Why was Peter surprised that Jesus wanted to wash his feet?

Walking in Love

what you need ✏

- Crayons or markers
- Scissors
- Stapler

what you do ✂

Before class, photocopy this page, making one for each child.

what children do ✋

1. Color the feet.
2. Put the feet in order with the cover on top.
3. Staple the feet together at the heel.
4. Write a reason you love Jesus each day this week. Keep this booklet as a reminder to walk with him.

what to say 📢

Jesus can help us with anything we need. He only asks us to have faith and love him in return.

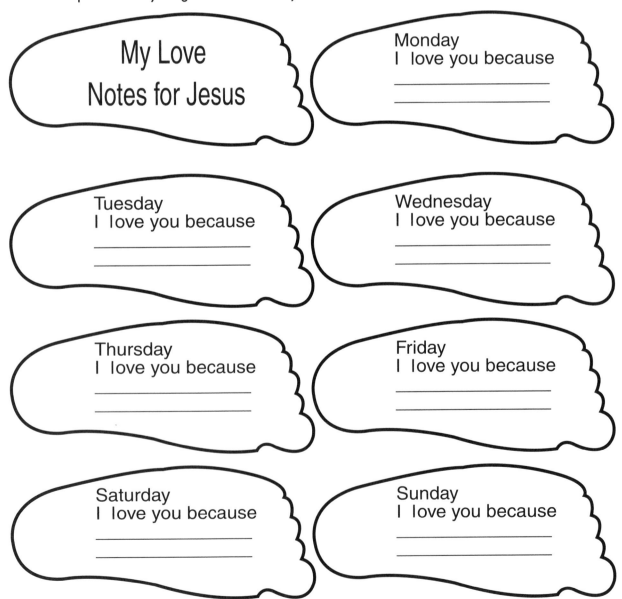

My Love
Notes for Jesus

Monday
I love you because
_____
_____

Tuesday
I love you because
_____
_____

Wednesday
I love you because
_____
_____

Thursday
I love you because
_____
_____

Friday
I love you because
_____
_____

Saturday
I love you because
_____
_____

Sunday
I love you because
_____
_____

Serving Others Like Jesus

what you need 🖌

- Crayons or markers
- Scissors
- Glue

what you do ✂

Before class, photocopy this page, making one for each child.

what children do ✋

1. Fill in the blanks on the arm. Write in who you will serve and how you will serve them.
2. Color and cut out the hand and arm templates.
3. Glue the hand to the arm by attaching the tab on the hand under the arm.

what to say 📢

Jesus showed love to his disciples by serving them. Even though he is our King, he serves us, too, because he loves us. Show someone you love them by serving them this week.

hand

arm

I PROMISE TO SHOW MY LOVE
TO _____ BY

_____

Deeds for Jesus

what you need 🖌

- Scissors
- Crayons or markers

what you do ✂

Before class, photocopy this page, making one for each child.

what children do ✋

1. Cut out the chart with the picture of Jesus.
2. Write your name at the top of the chart and color the picture of Jesus with his towel and basin.
3. Try to record a good deed you do for someone each day. Can you do this for a whole month?

what to say 📢

Jesus showed the disciples he loved them by serving them. How can you serve others this week?

Sunday	Monday	Tuesday	Wednesday	Thursday	Friday	Saturday

Jesus Washes the Disciples' Feet

An Example to Follow (based on John 13:1–17)

memory verse 📖

Serve one another in love.

Galatians 5:13

discussion questions 💬

1. Why did Jesus wash his disciples' feet?
2. Why was Peter surprised that Jesus wanted to wash his feet?

Serving Charades

Jesus showed love to his disciples by serving them. We can serve others just like Jesus did. Gather your friends or family members for a game of charades to see some good ways of serving others.

1. Color and cut out the charade pieces.
2. Fold the pieces in half and place them into a bowl.
3. Divide into two teams.
4. To play, have one person from the first team pick a charade. That player has 1 or 2 minutes to stand up and communicate the love charade without saying a word.
5. If the team guesses it, they get to keep the points for that charade. If not, the other team has a chance to guess the charade.
6. Continue taking turns until the charades have all been acted out. The team with the most points answers a discussion question.
7. When you use all the charade pieces, try to think of your own ways of serving people to continue playing.

Jesus Serves the Last Supper

memory verse 📖

[Jesus said,] "This is my body, which is given for you. Do this in remembrance of me."
Luke 22:19

To Remember Jesus (based on Luke 22:8–22)

It was time to celebrate the feast of Passover. Jesus sent some of his disciples to find a house to celebrate and to prepare the meal. Now, they were all gathered and ready to eat the delicious food before them.

"I have been very eager to eat this Passover meal with you before my suffering begins," Jesus told his disciples.

The disciples were confused. Why would Jesus be suffering?

Jesus continued by taking a filled cup from the table. Jesus prayed and thanked God for the drink. "Take this and share it among yourselves," Jesus said. "I will not drink again until the Kingdom of God has come."

After passing around the cup, Jesus took some bread from the table. He thanked God for the bread before breaking it into pieces. As he passed the pieces to each disciple, he said, "This is my body, which is given for you. Do this in remembrance of me."

Jesus told his disciples that the bread was his body. Then he said that the cup was his blood, and that it would be the new covenant between God and his people.

This was the last meal Jesus shared with his disciples before he died on the cross. Today, we remember this meal in church by having communion, or the Lord's Supper. It helps us remember that Jesus gave up his life on the cross to save us from our sins.

discussion

questions 💬

1. What were Jesus and his disciples celebrating?
2. What did the drink and the bread symbolize?

What Came First

what you need ✎

- Crayons or markers

what you do ✂

Before class, photocopy this page, making one for each child.

what children do ✋

1. Color the pictures.
2. Number the pictures in the correct order to tell the story of the Last Supper.

Hidden Room

what you need ✎

- Crayons or markers

what you do ✂

Before class, photocopy this page, making one for each child.

what children do ✋

1. Find the eight letters hidden around the room.
2. Unscramble the letters on the lines below to see what Jesus told his disciples to do at the Last Supper.
3. Color the picture.

____ _____

Last Supper Search

what you need ✏

- Crayons or markers

what you do ✂

Before class, photocopy this page, making one for each child.

what children do ✋

1. Circle the words in all capital letters in the story.

Each YEAR, the Jews had a special SUPPER, called the PASSOVER FEAST. JESUS and his DISCIPLES MET IN AN upper ROOM for their supper. Jesus TOOK WATER and WASHED his disciples' FEET. As they ate the MEAL, he TOLD them it would be his LAST ONE before he SUFFERED. He KNEW he was going TO DIE soon. He also said PETER would DENY him. Peter said he would never DO that, but he did.

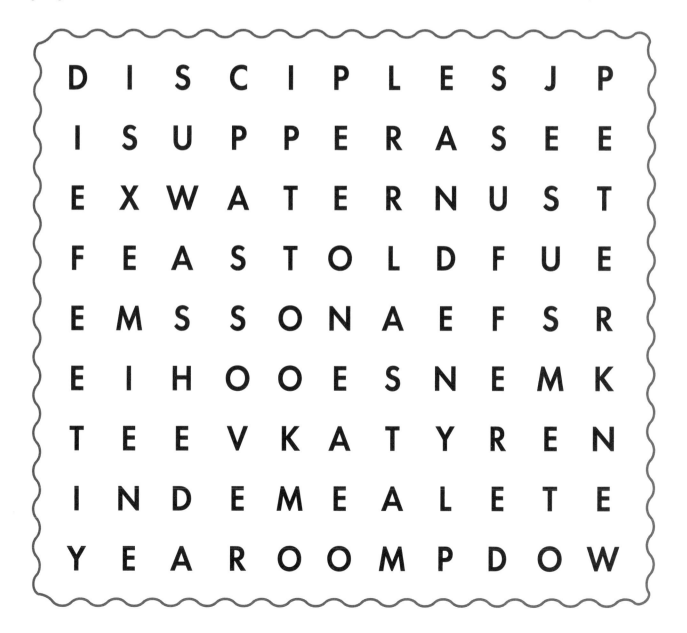

```
D I S C I P L E S J P
I S U P P E R A S E E
E X W A T E R N U S T
F E A S T O L D F U E
E M S S O N A E F S R
E I H O O E S N E M K
T E E V K A T Y R E N
I N D E M E A L E T E
Y E A R O O M P D O W
```

Jesus Serves the Last Supper

To Remember Jesus (based on Luke 22:8–22)

memory verse 📖

[Jesus said,] "This is my body, which is given for you. Do this in remembrance of me."
Luke 22:19

discussion questions 💬

1. What were Jesus and his disciples celebrating?
2. What did the drink and the bread symbolize?

A Special Meal

1. Cut out the pictures and glue them on a paper plate to serve at Jesus' special supper.
2. Combine 2½ cups flour, ½ cup salt, 1¾ cups boiling water, and 2 teaspoons vegetable oil.
3. Allow to cool slightly and knead until smooth. Store in airtight containers.
4. Mold the play clay into food shapes and let it harden uncovered over night. Use the pictures to guide you. (Do not eat the clay.)
5. Glue the food on the paper plate.

Jesus Dies

memory verse

God loved the world: He gave his one and only Son.
John 3:16

A Very Sad Day (based on John 19; Luke 23:26–56)

Jesus spent his life on Earth preaching and teaching the Good News about God. He told people that he had come to give them a new life. At first, not everyone understood what Jesus meant by this. When Jesus died on the cross, they finally understood.

Many of the religious leaders did not like that Jesus said he was God's Son, so they had him arrested. A ruler named Pilate said Jesus had to die on a heavy wooden cross. The people who didn't like Jesus shouted, "Crucify him," even though Jesus hadn't done anything wrong.

Roman soldiers whipped Jesus, put a crown of thorns on his head, and made him carry his cross to the hill where he would die. A man named Simon helped Jesus carry his cross when he became too weak to do it himself.

They hung Jesus on a cross next to two criminals. When Jesus was on the cross, he asked God to forgive the people who put him there. He knew that his death was all part of God's plan, and they didn't know what they were doing.

Finally, Jesus said, "It is finished!" Then, he took his final breath. Jesus' friends and family buried him in a nearby tomb. They were so sad that Jesus died! But they wouldn't be sad for long. God had a plan.

God loves us so much that he sent his own son to Earth to die for us. Jesus died to pay the price for our sins. If we believe in Jesus, then we are forgiven when we do wrong things. We can be happy because Jesus' sacrifice saved us from our sins.

discussion questions

1. How did Jesus die?
2. Why did Jesus have to die?

What Happened Next

what you need ✏
- Crayons or markers

what you do ✂
Before class, photocopy this page, making one for each child.

what children do 🖐
1. Draw a line to match the statements so they make sense.

what to say 📢
Jesus died for all of our sins. It's important that we remember his sacrifice so we always know how much Jesus loves us. Can you remember the story of Jesus' crucifixion? Try to match each statement to see what happened next in the story.

Pilate sentenced   carry his cross.

The soldiers   was placed on Jesus' head.

A crown of thorns   Jesus to be crucified.

Jesus carried his   my sins.

Simon helped Jesus   gave Jesus a beating.

Jesus died for   cross until he fell.

 Top 50 Bible Stories about Jesus for Elementary.

Forgiveness Wreath

what you need ✎
- Crayons or markers
- Scissors
- Glue

what you do ✂
Before class, photocopy this page, making one for each child.

what children do ✋
1. Color and cut out each cross and the "I Forgive" circle.
2. Glue crosses around the edge of the circle to make a wreath.

what to say 📢
Jesus died on the cross for everyone, giving us forgiveness for our sins even though we don't deserve it. Do you find it hard to forgive those who hurt you? Maybe your sister breaks your favorite toy, your friend says unkind things about you, or the neighborhood bully pushes your bike over, causing it to get scratched. It's not always easy to forgive!

I
Forgive

John 19

Jesus Died for All

what you need ✒

- Crayons or markers
- Timer

what you do ✂

Before class, photocopy this page, making one for each child. During class, tell children how much time they have when start. Set a timer for the given time. When time is up, ask children to read their lists.

what children do ✋

1. When given the signal, make as many words as you can out of the letters HE DIED FOR ALL in the time given. Print the words on the lines.

Jesus Dies

A Very Sad Day (based on John 19; Luke 23:26–56)

memory verse 📖

God loved the world: He gave his one and only Son.
John 3:16

discussion questions 💬

1. How did Jesus die?
2. Why did Jesus have to die?

Cross Paperweight

1. Find a rock with a mostly flat bottom.
2. Paint the rock or decorate it with glue and glitter.
3. While the rock is drying, color and cut out the cross.
4. Once the rock is dry, place the rock on a table, flat side down.
5. Tape the cross to the side of the rock, using the rock as a stand.
6. Keep your paperweight to remind you of Jesus' sacrifice.

Jesus Is Alive!

memory verse 📖

The Lord has really risen!
Luke 24:34

The Empty Tomb (based on Matthew 27:57–66; 28:1–10)

After Jesus died on the cross, his friends and family buried him in a tomb. They wrapped his body in a long white sheet of linen and then rolled a giant rock in front of the tomb. Guards watched the tomb day and night to make sure no one bothered Jesus' body.

Before Jesus died, he told his followers that he would come back to life after three days. They were almost too sad to believe this after watching him die. On the third day, though, the promise came true!

Two women went to visit Jesus' tomb. When they arrived, they felt an earthquake! An angel had rolled away the stone blocking the tomb! The angel's face was bright and shiny.

"Don't be afraid," the angel said. "Jesus isn't here! He is risen from the dead, just as he said would happen."

The women went into the tomb and saw that Jesus was really gone!

"Go quickly and tell his disciples that he has risen from the dead," the angel continued. "You can find him in Galilee."

The women ran from the tomb to tell the disciples this wonderful news. On their way, they saw Jesus! They stopped and worshiped him. They were so happy to see Jesus.

Finally, the women made it back to Jesus' disciples. They could hardly believe the good news. They left at once to find Jesus.

discussion questions 💬

1. How long was Jesus dead?
2. Who told the women that Jesus was alive?

Gold Cross Wall Hanging

what you need 🖌

- Scissors
- Gold foil
- Glue
- Black construction paper

- Crayons or markers
- Confetti or other small pieces of colored paper

- Hole punch
- Yarn

what you do ✂

Before class, photocopy this page, making one for each child. Cut squares of gold foil.

what children do ✋

1. Cut out the window.
2. Fold the window in half and cut out the cross.
3. Unfold the window and glue gold foil on the back.
4. Glue the window onto black construction paper and cut a frame around the window.
5. Color and glue on confetti or other colored paper onto the window
6. Punch a hole in the top and insert a yarn hanger.

Resurrection Puzzle

what you need

- Crayons or markers
- Scissors
- Glue
- Construction paper

what you do ✂

Before class, photocopy this page, making one for each child.

what children do 🖐

1. Color and cut out the picture.
2. Glue the picture onto construction paper.
3. Cut out each section of the picture to make a puzzle.
4. Try putting together the puzzle with the colored side up. Then try it with the construction paper side up.

Complete the Picture

what you need 🖌

- Crayons or markers

what you do ✂

Before class, photocopy this page, making one for each child.

what children do ✋

1. Complete the scene of Jesus' empty tomb. Draw an angel telling the women the good news.
2. Draw the women looking surprised when they hear what happened.
3. Color the picture.

Jesus Is Alive!

The Empty Tomb (based on Matthew 27:57–66; 28:1–10)

memory verse 📖

The Lord has really risen!
Luke 24:34

discussion questions 💬

1. How long was Jesus dead?
2. Who told the women that Jesus was alive?

Easter Story in Code

See if you can read the story in code. Maybe you can read it to a friend who does not know the real Easter message. Say a prayer that God will help you as you read this story to your friend.

At  the came 2 the . They said, "Who will

roll the away 4 us?" When they looked, the was rolled away!

An  inside the said, "B not afraid. Jesus is risen!

Look at this MT ! Go and tell that Jesus is risen. U will C him

there." The  was right, Jesus is alive!

Jesus Visits Thomas

memory verse 📖

Blessed are those who believe without seeing me.
John 20:29

Thomas Wants to See (based on John 20:19–31)

After Jesus had died and risen again, the disciples held a meeting in someone's home. They locked all the doors and windows because they were afraid of the people who had killed Jesus.

The disciples were all talking amongst themselves. Suddenly, Jesus appeared! He was standing right in front of them!

"Peace be with you," Jesus said, showing the disciples the wounds on his hands and sides from the cross.

The disciples were thrilled to see Jesus.

One of the disciples, Thomas, was not in the room when Jesus came. When the disciples told Thomas what had happened, he didn't believe them.

"I won't believe it unless I see the nail wounds in his hands," Thomas said.

Later, the disciples met again. This time, Thomas was with them. Suddenly, Jesus appeared again!

Jesus said to Thomas, "Put your finger here, and look at my hands. Don't be faithless any longer."

Thomas was amazed by what he saw.

Jesus turned again to Thomas and said, "You believe because you have seen me. Blessed are those who believe without seeing me."

We might not be able to see Jesus today. But that doesn't mean that we can't believe in him! That's why we have to have faith. Faith is believing in things that we can't see.

discussion questions 💬

1. Why didn't Thomas believe the other disciples had seen Jesus?
2. What is faith?

Faith Hands

what you need ✎

- Scissors
- Crayons or markers

what you do ✂

Before class, photocopy this page, making one for each child.

what children do ✋

1. Cut out the hand templates.
2. Color each hand. Draw a hole in each hand to show Jesus' wounds.
3. Turn over the hands to the blank side. On one hand, write the word *Faith*. Write this week's memory verse on the other hand (*Blessed are those who believe without seeing me.* John 20:29)

what to say 📢

Thomas didn't believe Jesus had returned until he saw him in person. Jesus wanted Thomas to have more faith, so he would believe in him. Faith is believing in things we cannot see. We can't see Jesus, but we can still have faith and believe in him.

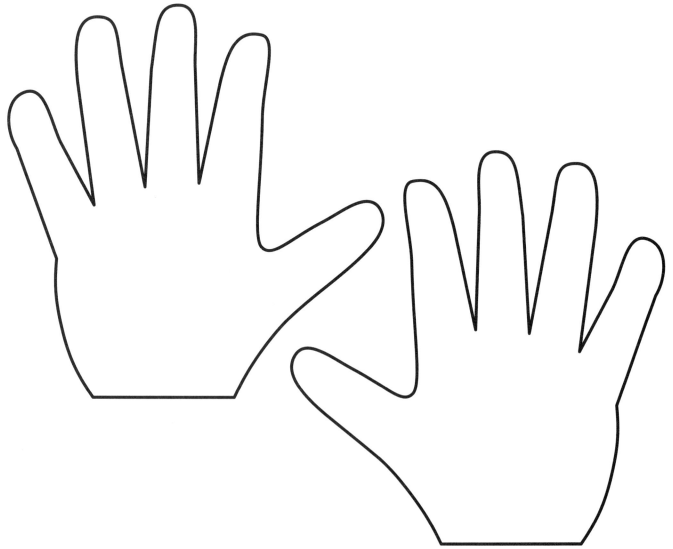

Fill in the Bandage

what you need ✎

- Crayons or markers
- Adhesive bandages

what you do ✂

Before class, photocopy this page, making one for each child.

what children do ✋

1. Color the picture.
2. Draw nail wounds on Jesus' hands.
3. Put an adhesive bandage on Jesus' side.
4. Fill in the missing words in the memory verse.

"Blessed are those who

__ __ __ __ __ __ __ __"

John 20:29

Faith Code

what you need ✎

- Crayons or markers

what you do ✂

Before class, photocopy this page, making one for each child.

what children do ✋

1. What did Jesus say to Thomas when he returned? Crack the code below to find out.

what to say 🔊

We don't have to see Jesus to believe in him. We can have faith that he lives!

Code:	Q	W	E	R	T	Y	U	I	O	P	A	S	D	F	G	H	J	K	L	Z	X	C	V	B	N	M
Letter:	A	B	C	D	E	F	G	H	I	J	K	L	M	N	O	P	Q	R	S	T	U	V	W	X	Y	Z

W S T L L T R   Q K T

Z I G L T   V I G

W T S O T C T

V O Z I G X Z

L T T O F U D T.

P G I F **20:29**

Jesus Visits Thomas

Thomas Wants to See (based on John 20:19–31)

memory verse

Blessed are those who believe without seeing me.
John 20:29

discussion questions

1. Why didn't Thomas believe the other disciples had seen Jesus?
2. What is faith?

Faith Puzzle

It might not look like it, but you can make the puzzle below into several different things. Can you make something new from the puzzle without looking at the possibilities? Or do you need help to see, like Thomas? Jesus told Thomas to have faith—to believe in him without seeing him.

1. Color and cut out the puzzle.
2. Try arranging the puzzle into new shapes. Look at the Puzzle Possibilities if you need help.

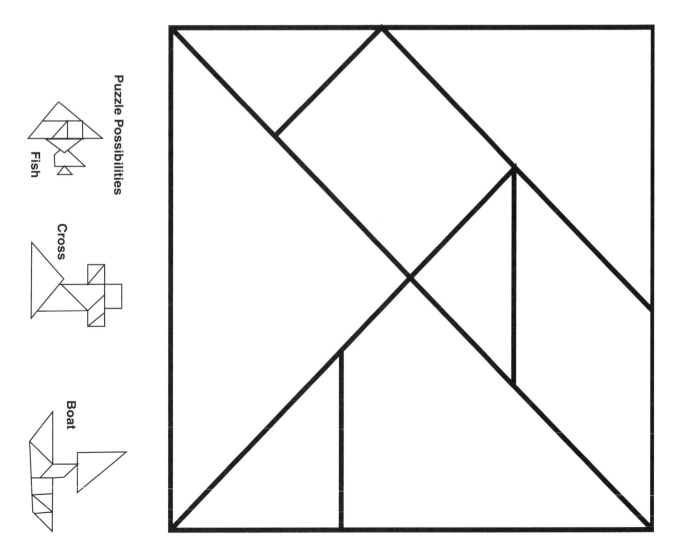

Puzzle Possibilities

Fish

Cross

Boat

Breakfast with Jesus

memory verse 📖

The LORD is good to those who depend on him.
Lamentations 3:25

Plenty of Fish (based on John 21:1–14)

After Jesus died and rose again, he appeared to his disciples several times before going back to Heaven.

Once, several of Jesus' disciples decided to go fishing. They set out in their boat and fished all night, but they didn't catch anything.

At dawn, they saw someone standing on the beach. They couldn't tell who he was, but he was calling out to them.

"Have you caught any fish?" The stranger asked.

When the disciples said no, the man told them to toss the net on the right-hand side of the boat. The disciples did as they were told. When they pulled the net back in, it was filled with fish! It was too heavy to bring onto the boat!

Suddenly, the disciples realized that the stranger on the beach wasn't a stranger at all. It was Jesus! When Peter, one of Jesus' disciples, realized, he jumped into the water and swam to shore while the others brought the boat in.

When they made it to the shore, Jesus had a breakfast of bread and fish cooked over a fire waiting for them. Jesus served his disciples breakfast, and they all enjoyed the morning together.

discussion questions 💬

1. How did Peter respond when he saw Jesus?
2. How did Jesus provide for the disciples?

Plenty of Provision

what you need ✏

- Crayons or markers
- Scissors
- Tape

what you do ✂

Before class, photocopy this page, making one for each child.

what children do ✋

1. Color and write your name on one side of each fish.
2. Cut out the fish.
3. Fold each fish on the dashed line.
4. Is there a way Jesus has provided for you lately? Write a prayer on the inside of each fish thanking Jesus for his provision.
5. Tape the fish together at their tail fins.

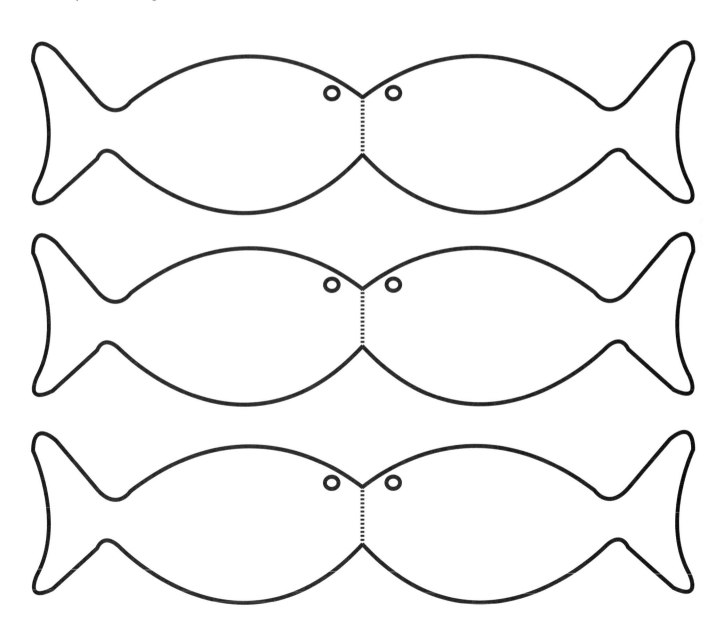

Seek-And-Find Fish

what you need ✎

- Colored paper
- Scissors
- Marker

what you do ✂

Before class, photocopy this page onto colored paper. Cut out each fish. Write a discussion question on the back of two of the fish. On the third fish, write, "Recite the memory verse." Hide the fish around the room.

what children do ✋

1. Search the room to find the three missing fish.
2. When you find a fish, take it to your teacher.
3. Complete the task on the back of the fish.

Confusing Fishing

what you need 🖌

- Crayons or markers

what you do ✂

Before class, photocopy this page, making one for each child.

what children do ✋

1. Color the fish according to the math codes. Each color is represented by a number.
2. Complete the math problem. The number answer will tell you what color to use. For example, seven minus five equals two. Color the fin orange because it is the number two color.

what to say 📢

The disciples hadn't caught any fish all night. They were confused when the stranger told them to throw their nets on the other side of the boat. But the advice worked! Jesus' ways might not make sense to us, but they always succeed. Don't get confused by these math problems! If you figure them out, you'll succeed in creating a colorful fish!

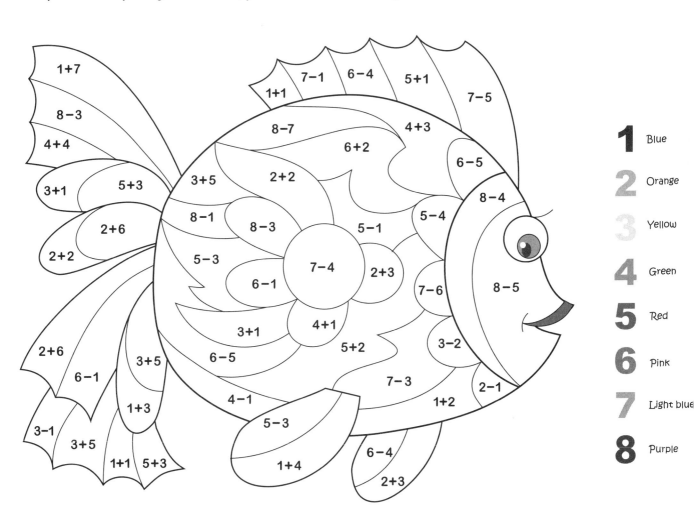

1 Blue
2 Orange
3 Yellow
4 Green
5 Red
6 Pink
7 Light blue
8 Purple

Breakfast with Jesus

Plenty of Fish (based on John 21:1–14)

memory verse 📖

The LORD is good to those who depend on him.
Lamentations 3:25

discussion questions 💬

1. How did Peter respond when he saw Jesus?
2. How did Jesus provide for the disciples?

Crispy Cereal Balls

When the disciples met Jesus on the shore, he had breakfast waiting for them. Follow this recipe to make breakfast for someone you love.

Crispy Cereal Balls

1. Mix these ingredients together in a bowl:
   - ½ cup peanut butter
   - ½ cup flaked coconut
   - ½ cup honey
   - ½ cup chopped peanuts

2. Add ½ cup crispy rice cereal to those ingredients and mix.

3. In a separate flat dish, place 1 ½ cups crispy rice cereal.

4. Scoop out large spoonfuls of the peanut butter mixture and form it into balls.

5. Roll the balls in the cereal until covered.

6. While you eat the crispy cookies, talk about Jesus' breakfast with his disciples from John 21:1–14.

Jesus Is with Us

memory verse

[Jesus said,] "I am with you always, even to the end of the age."
Matthew 28:20

An Important Job (based on Matthew 28:18–20)

Even after Jesus died, his disciples weren't alone. Jesus rose from the tomb, and he visited his friends a few more times before going back to Heaven. During one of his last visits, Jesus gave his disciples an important job.

"Go and make disciples of all the nations," Jesus told his disciples. "Baptize them in the name of the Father and the Son and the Holy spirit."

A disciple is someone who learns from someone else. Jesus' disciples learned from him. Now it was their job to make even more disciples.

"Teach these new disciples to obey all the commands I have given you," Jesus said.

Jesus' disciples knew they had been given an important task. Since Jesus was going back to Heaven, they had to keep doing what Jesus had taught them on Earth!

Some of them might have been scared. But Jesus reassured them.

"Don't worry," Jesus said. "I am with you always, even to the end of the age."

We call this the great commission. Jesus told his disciples to find other people and make them his disciples, too. And that job didn't end with the disciples! With Jesus' help, you and I can make new disciples for Jesus today.

discussion questions

1. What is a disciple?
2. What is the great commission?

Salvation Plan Booklet

what you need ✎

- Crayons or markers
- Scissors
- Paper
- Stapler

what you do ✂

Before class, photocopy this page, making one for each child.

what children do ✋

1. Color and cut out the "Go" box.
2. Trace the "Go" box four times onto a piece of paper and cut out each piece.
3. Write one step to salvation on each page and add an appropriate design or picture.
4. Stack the papers in order, with the "Go" box on top as a cover.
5. Staple the papers together on the left side at the top and bottom to make a booklet.

The Plan of Salvation

1. God loves us.
~ 1 John 4:10

2. We are separated from God's love because we do wrong things (sin).
~ Romans 3:23

3. Even though sin brings death, God sent his Son to take the punishment for us.
~ Romans 6:23; 1 John 4:9-10

4. To accept God's plan of salvation for us, we must pray, admitting our sins to God and asking Jesus to be our Savior.
~ 2 John 1:9; Romans 10:9; Acts 16:31

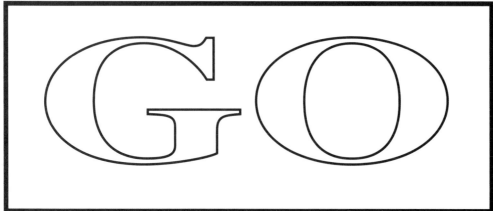

Time to Tell Clock

what you need 🖌

- Crayons or markers
- Scissors
- Paper fasteners
- Construction paper
- Glue

what you do ✂

Before class, photocopy this page, making one for each child.

what children do ✋

1. Color and cut out the clock and hands.
2. Write the remaining numbers on the clock.
3. Attach the hands to the clock with a paper fastener.
4. Fold a piece of construction paper in half and glue the clock to the front, as shown, to make it stand up.

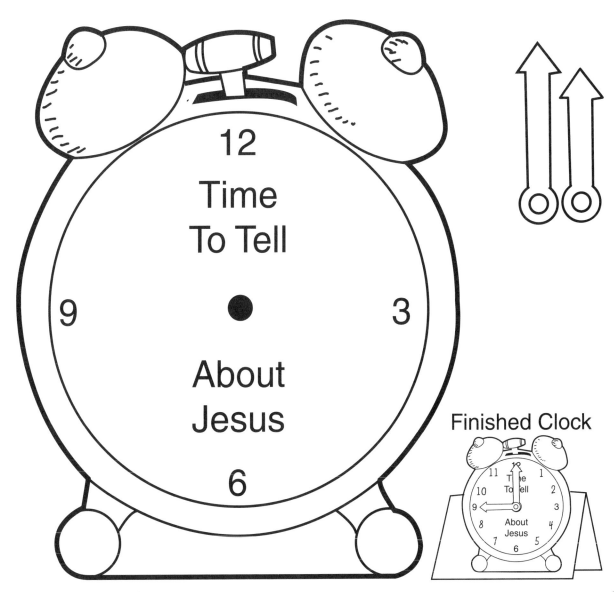

Finished Clock

Messenger for Jesus

what you need ✎

- Crayons or markers

what you do ✂

Before class, photocopy this page, making one for each child.

what children do ✋

1. Make this messenger's face look as much like you as you can. Draw on hair that looks like yours. Add your eyes, nose, and smile. Write your name on the hat. Get ready, like a messenger, to tell the Good News.

what to say 📢

Jesus gave a wonderful message for the disciples and us to tell others. We are to tell the Good News that God loves us and that Jesus died for us. He wants to be our Savior. Be like a messenger and tell the Good News of Jesus!

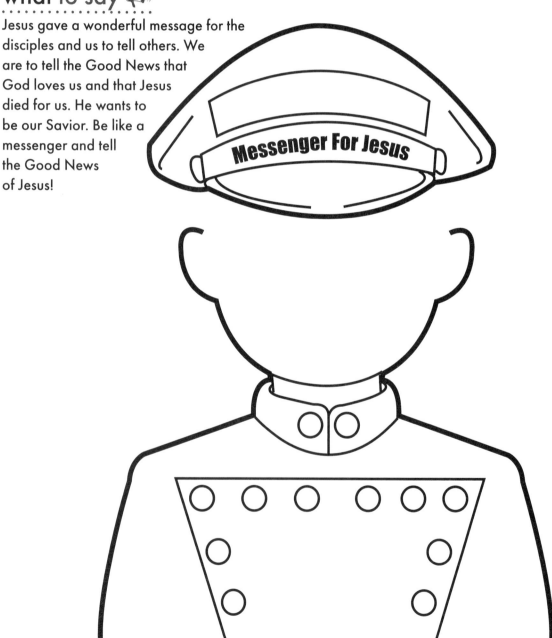

Messenger For Jesus

Jesus Is with Us

An Important Job (based on Matthew 28:18–20)

memory verse 📖

[Jesus said,] "I am with you always, even to the end of the age."
Matthew 28:20

discussion questions 💬

1. What is a disciple?
2. What is the great commission?

Mirror Message

What words do you think were the most helpful to the disciples as Jesus left? Read the message below and see if you can tell what they were. Then, on the blank spaces, write the backward Bible words forward. Use a mirror to help decipher the message.

> I AM WITH YOU ALWAYS, EVEN TO THE END OF HTE AGE.
> MATTHEW 28:20

DISCIPLES

_____

JESUS

_____

LAZARUS

_____

RESURRECTION

_____

SAVIOR

_____

BETHLEHEM

_____

NATIONS

_____

GALILEE

_____

Jesus' Heavenly Home

memory verse

[Jesus said,] "I am going to prepare a place for you."
John 14:2

Jesus Returns Home (based on John 14:1–3; Acts 1:6–12)

Jesus was on Earth for forty days after he rose from the dead. He used this time to comfort and teach his disciples so they would be ready to spread the Good News.

Finally, it was time for Jesus to return to Heaven. Jesus' disciples and friends were sad at first. They wanted Jesus to stay with them on Earth forever. But that wasn't God's plan.

"Don't let your hearts be troubled," Jesus said. "You can trust in God, and you can trust in me. I'm going back to my Father's house, where there is plenty of room. I'm going to prepare a place for you there."

Jesus' Father's house is Heaven. His followers were happy to know that they would be together again someday. They were also happy to know that Jesus wasn't leaving forever.

"When everything is ready," Jesus continued, "I will come and get you, so that you will always be with me. Only God knows when that will be, but keep spreading the Good News until then. You will be my witness, telling people about me everywhere."

When Jesus was done speaking, the disciples watched as he went into Heaven on a cloud, all the way up until they could no longer see him. Jesus was home in Heaven, and they would be ready for him when he returned.

discussion questions

1. What did Jesus ask his disciples to do before he went to Heaven?
2. What do you think Heaven is like?

A Special Promise Pennant

what you need ✎

- Crayons or markers
- Scissors
- Construction paper
- Glue
- Tape
- Plastic straws

what you do ✂

Before class, photocopy this page, making one for each child.

what children do 🖐

1. Color and cut out the pennant.
2. Cut small confetti shapes out of construction paper and glue to the pennant around the letters.
3. Tape a straw to the back of the pennant.
4. Hang somewhere to remind you of Jesus' promise.

what to say 📢

Jesus was on Earth for forty days after he rose from the dead. His disciples wanted him to stay with them forever, but Jesus needed to go back to Heaven. This pennant will remind you of his promise to return.

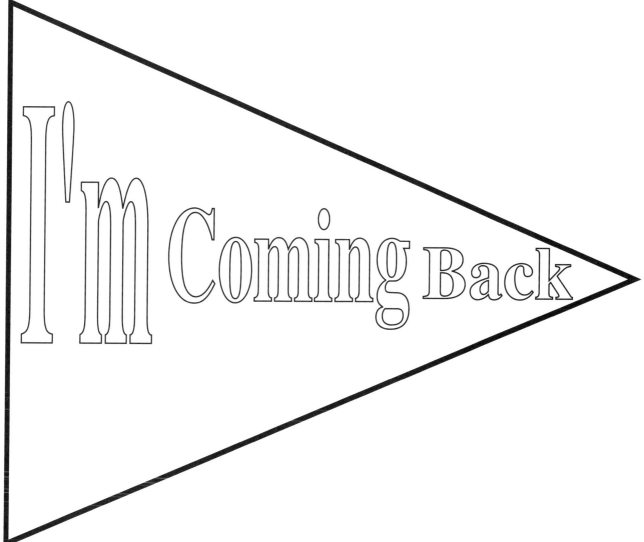

Thank You, Jesus

what you need

- Crayons or markers
- Glue
- Cotton balls

what you do ✂

Before class, photocopy this page, making one for each child.

what children do ✋

1. Color the picture of Jesus.
2. Glue cotton balls to the cloud.
3. Write a prayer of thankfulness to Jesus on the lines next to the picture.

what to say 📣

Jesus died, but he rose again. After living on Earth for forty days, he returned to Heaven to prepare a place for us to live with him for eternity. Write a prayer thanking Jesus for preparing a place for you.

_____

_____

_____

_____

_____

_____

_____

Heavenly Mobile

what you need 🖌

- Scissors
- Glue
- Cotton balls
- Hole punch
- Yarn
- Plastic straws

what you do ✂

Before class, photocopy this page, making one for each child.

what children do 🖐

1. Cut out the clouds.
2. Glue cotton balls around the edges.
3. Punch holes in the top and tie a piece of yarn to each cloud.
4. Tie a loop to the other end of the yarn and insert a plastic straw through the loops to make a mobile.

what to say 📢

Jesus' work on Earth was done. He returned to heaven to live and reign with God, his Father. He promised to come back someday. If we believe in him, he will take us to Heaven to live with him.

Jesus went to Heaven.

Jesus reigns in Heaven with God.

Jesus is coming back someday.

finished craft

Jesus' Heavenly Home

Jesus Returns Home (based on John 14:1–3; Acts 1:6–12)

memory verse 📖

[Jesus said,] "I am going to prepare a place for you."
John 14:2

discussion questions 💬

1. What did Jesus ask his disciples to do before he went to Heaven?
2. What do you think Heaven is like?

Preparing a Place

1. Write the memory verse on the lines below Jesus.
2. Glue cotton balls to the clouds.
3. Color the picture.

John 14:2